Comment on the English Edition

It was not until she met Jonathan and Rusky in *The Brothers Lionheart* that Shiori Sato became captured by Astrid Lindgren's stories. Shiori had not found some of the other characters in Lindgren's books, such as Pippi Longstocking, that interesting. Pippi is strong and happy with her life. She will never grow up to become an adult. The characters that Shiori finds most interesting are children that have difficulties in their real lives, but who can be happy in their dreams. They go to a dream world and they never comes back to their real lives. In their dreams they are princes and they become strong. They can fight against evil and they can win in the end.

Shiori analyzes Lindgren's stories of children taking refuge in a dream world, in the light of relations between fathers and sons or between brothers. She compares these stories with the tale of the two brothers Baldur and Hodur in Norse Mythology. Shiori has studied Lindgren's life and she can see Lindgren's sorrow over lost family members reflected in these books.

Shiori provides an interesting analysis, which can offer a different perspective, specially to the character of Rusky, when one goes back and re-reads *The Brothers Lionheart*.

—**Keiko Sampei**, author of *Astrid Lindgren, the Creator of Pippi* **(a Lindgren´s biography)**

Becoming Free

BECOMING FREE

Essays in Criticism on Children's Literature
—Books That Encourage Us—

Shiori Sato

Translated by
Ritsuko Hirose

TERRAINC
KAWASAKI

Originally published in Japanese in 2013 by Terrainc, Kawasaki, under the title *Jiyu ni Natteiku*.

Published by Terrainc, Inc, 14–7, Mukaibara 3-chome, Asao-ku Kawasaki-shi, Kanagawa 215–0007.

Copyright © 2013 by Shiori Sato.
English translation copyright © 2016 by Ritsuko Hirose.
All rights reserved. Printed in Japan.

First edition, 2016
ISBN978-4-86261-123-9

www.terrainc.co.jp

Dedicated to
late Prof. Hayao Kawai

Contents

Foreword—Gaining a New Sense Organ   xi

Chapter I
To Live in Belief   —*The Silver Coach*—   1

Chapter II
Seeking for an Eternal Companion   —from *Emily, the Liar*—   6

Chapter III
What Mice Suggest to Us
—The Creatures That Dwell in Another World—   13

Chapter IV
Imagination and Freedom   —Ability the Mousewife Acquired—   23

Chapter V
From Being a Benefactor to Being a Friend   —*The Cat Visitor*—   38

Chapter VI
Longing for Eternity   I
—What Has Arisen from the World of Lindgren's Works—   41

Chapter VII
Longing for Eternity   II   —"The Eternal Child" in Lindgren—   49

Chapter VIII
Building Up an Image of an Independent Woman
—What Does *The Yearling* Mean to Rawlings?—   59

Chapter IX
The Ability of Severance and the Future   —*Ai's Left Side*—   72

Chapter X
In the Garden of Integration and Restoration
—What Is the Significance of *The Secret Garden* to Burnett?—   84

Chapter XI
The Two in the Haze   —Why was *Peter Pan* Born?—   99

Chapter XII
From an Incomprehensible Story to a Comprehensible Story
—*Tom's Midnight Garden* by Philippa Pearce—   113

Chapter XIII
The Negative Aspects in Human Nature
—Comparing the Two Editions of Japanese Translation of
The Hundred Dresses by Eleanor Estes—   126

Chapter XIV
The Man Who Wanted to Become a King
—*The Little Prince* and *The Wisdom of the Sands* as Its Parent Body—   132

The List of the First Appearance   147
Afterword—Children's Literature for Adults   148
To the English Edition   150
Afterword by the Translator   152

Foreword—Gaining a New Sense Organ

In 1996, I began studying at The Center for Research in Picture Books and Children's Literature, located in Otaru, Hokkaido, north Japan. The next June, I became a member of a society for research in children's literature, Maho-no-Empitsu [Magic Pencil]. I revised my short criticism titled "To live in belief," which I had submitted to the competition run by the Center, and contributed it to the Vol. 16 of the bulletin published by Maho-no-Empitsu. While the members of the society were writers, illustrators of picture books and poets, I wrote only criticism.

Although it is difficult to describe in a word what criticism means, I think that criticism is a bridge between the texts and the readers. And the purpose of criticism is to clarify the value of the creation and show it to both the writer and the reader.

Each of my critical works was my harvest for the year. I have long had a strong sense that I have always been searching for something within myself. Once I have organized my thought in writing a criticism, my heart settles for a moment. But it is only for a moment and then I feel urged to pursue another theme. I will keep writing as long as I feel this sense of being compelled. I might have gradually developed a new sense organ while writing a criticism. In *The Mousewife*, the novel I love most, what the mouse acquired might be regarded as being in a sphere of her own and knowing her own position in the world, which are goals toward which I feel myself clearing a path to become free. The top of my desk is overflowing with many books, notebooks and materials and is never tidied up. While I feel sorry for my family, I am really happy and grateful that I can continue to do and seek for what I like to do.

It has long been my dream to publish a book of criticism. In realizing my dream, I owe much to my family and to my companions and friends who are bound by strong ties of "books." I would like to express heartfelt appreciations to Ms. Sayuri Yamada, an illustrator, who encouraged me to move forwards, Ms. Masako Fujiki, my best friend, who has set up my manuscripts for printing for a long time, and my son, Mr. Kai Sato. I wish to thank all concerned from the bottom of my heart.

I feel frightened as well as excited to imagine the way this book will be read by you, who will happen to take it in your hand.

Shiori Sato,
March 2013

Chapter I

To Live in Belief
—*The Silver Coach*—

Carole S. Adler
The Silver Coach
New York: Coward, McCann & Geoghegan, 1979

* Japanese edition: Adler, Carole S. *Gin no Basha*. Trans. Yoshiko Tarusawa. Illus. Kenji Kitagawa. Tokyo: Kin no Hoshi Sha, 1983.

What was I born for? This question might have been asked by each of us at least once. It can be said that human beings live with this question in mind whether consciously or unconsciously. I strongly desire to find the answer to this question. The belief that my life should be meaningful and that I will discover what I am meant to do gives me hope. To live seems to be to continuously sustain an emotional hurt. Even in this predicament, children's literature has continued to supply hope to me. Reading children's literature has nurtured an ability in me to think deeply about the essence in things and the significance of my life.

In this chapter, I will consider this fundamental question, "What was I born for?" in the context of the relationships between the mothers and the children in C. S. Adler's *The Silver Coach* (1979). I will look at this theme from the perspective not of the protagonist, but of the secondly important character, Grandmother Wallace.

One day, the peacefulness of her life is broken. Wallace's granddaughters are left to her care during the summer. She had never seen them. The daughter-in-law, whom she has seen only once, has just got divorced from her son. Wallace notices soon that the mother and the elder granddaughter are not getting along well with each other; the mother who loves the child but cannot convey her love to her daughter well and the daughter who thinks she is not loved by her mother. They remind Wallace of the relationship between herself and her son.

Wallace has two children. The younger, a daughter, was mentally-disabled from birth and lived with her receiving care in a good environment in the countryside, and the elder, a son, was sent to a boarding school for his good education and had lived apart from his parents. It might be considered to be an appropriate decision by well-meaning parents. Her son grew up to be a healthy and naughty boy who sometimes gave trouble to the people around him. Meanwhile, her daughter could not live without her parents' care. Wallace loved this pitiful daughter deeply. She felt tranquility and joy in life with her daughter. Wallace was not unhappy, but this choice was the beginning of her long-lasting agony. A child always desires his or her parents' love strongly. Regardless of any handicap or the difference in age between the rival, a child wants his or her parents to love only him or her. Wallace's son was deeply hurt by the fact that his mother had not chosen him and he shut his heart. Self-accusation assailed her. Her conscience accused herself without mercy: Didn't I prefer my daughter, helpless, gentle and meek, than my son, self-centered and insensitive; can I deny that bias in me?

When a mother considers the relationships between herself and her children, this doubt might cross almost all mothers' minds. I have two sons. They differ in their character, taste and way of life. I love both, but I must admit that there is difference in the hint of my love to them depending on the ease in getting along and mutual-understanding. Affinity is another matter. It was natural that Wallace should choose her daughter. That choice to pursue a deeper happiness may have occurred unconsciously. However, Wallace, at her young age, could not think of it. As a result, a deep gap between the mother and the son emerged. And the gap has continued to vex Wallace and had been left untouched for ages.

It is at that time that the life with her granddaughters begins unexpectedly. Wallace's heart is stirred up. She thinks she must not leave the child as she is and that she must encourage the mother and the daughter to bridge the same gap that Wallace and her son had not. She realizes that she has encountered what she should do in her life. She begins to cautiously soften her granddaughter, Chris's heart. She tells her that everyone has strength and weakness and that what is important is not sweet words but to sympathize with others, to be honest and useful to others and to be confident in oneself. Her persistent persuasion heals Chris's wounds and helps her to mature little by little. Wallace pours all her strength into this endeavor and finally she succeeds in restoring the relationship between the mother and the daughter. After a long and painful period of introspection, a person, who has borne a deep wound in their heart in the past, accomplishes their own task by giving a hand to someone emotionally damaged. Wallace must have realized that she had lived for this moment. In order to be released from her own question, she needed to actually execute something. For even if time has power to heal injury, it failed to persuade her.

1. Something occurs.
2. A person-concerned is deeply injured.
3. The pain in them urges themselves to act.
4. Their heart is cured and they return to life.

However, the relationships between Wallace and her son have not changed. Isn't it possible for both of them to stretch their arms toward each other? In my view the relationships between parents and children are often too close and too entangled to be true to their emotion.

I will try to illustrate it in two examples as is done in *The Silver Coach*. Here I summarize the two stories.

In J. G. Robinson's *When Marnie Was There* (1967), Anna's late grandmother, Marnie, who was not loved by her parents in her childhood, appears as a girl in front of Anna, who is now an orphan. Marnie becomes Anna's friend, and cures her heart shut to the world. Marnie leads Anna to a wider and brighter world.

In the other story, K. Pearson's *A Handful of Time* (1987), the protagonist, finding an old pocket watch accidentally, witnesses episodes from her mother, Ruth's girlhood. Ruth was not loved by her mother. However, after seeing the past, the protagonist, who has always doubted her mother's love, feels deep sympathy for her mother, as she finally comes to know her mother's injured heart. This finding enhances the protagonist's love for her mother. It fills her mother, Ruth, with joy and the mother's heart is healed.

These works seem to show that the solution of problems concerning human's mind cannot be easily accomplished only by the people themselves. It may be needless to say that humans cannot re-start their life afresh, but what they can do is to make use of their experiences in their present and future life. When people meet another who has similar wounds in their heart as theirs and they can combine the meaning of their life with the solution of another's problem, then it would be possible for them to bring their own hearts to life.

In *The Silver Coach*, Wallace's son is building a new family. His natural cheerfulness covers his irresponsible attitude, but, in some way or other, it will be revealed to his wife and child. What will he do then? Will he try to make another family, or will someone in his family heal his wounds and revive his heart? Or the day might come when he himself will execute his power to cure someone else's heart.

With this thought in mind, it might be possible to believe that I will become useful in accomplishing some others' past task, or I may be doing it now. We, in our age, might be carrying unknowingly on our shoulders what people in the past who were afflicted with unhappy thoughts sought for, be driven by them, or be urged to choose something. At the same time, we ought to believe that the problems we are burdened with now could be solved by the next generation.

The strong desire by each person for finding the significance of life generates a positive activity in others, helps human beings continue to exist for generations and leads them to a better existence. This belief brings us to the notion that human beings influence each other and live supported by others in a long cycle and that humanity is worth believing in.

Works Consulted

Adler, Carole S. *The Silver Coach*. New York: Coward, McCann & Geoghegan, 1979.

---. *Gin no Basha* [The Silver Coach] 銀の馬車. Trans. Tarusawa Yoshiko 足沢良子. Tokyo: Kin no Hoshi Sha 金の星社, 1983.

Pearson, Kit. *A Handful of Time*. Markham, ON: Viking Kestrel, 1987.

Robinson, Joan G. *When Marnie Was There*. London: Collins, 1967.

Chapter II

Seeking for an Eternal Companion
—from *Emily, the Liar*—

Kiyo Shibamura
Usotsuki Emiri **[Emily, the Liar]**
Illustrated by Yuichi Yamamoto
Tokyo: Dainippon Tosho, 1996

I went out shopping downtown. My son, a junior-high student, accompanied me. I seldom go downtown, and I felt secure with a companion. I was relaxed, and the pleasure of going out arose naturally. Our everyday lives are often maintained by such support. But in a crucial moment, a human may make decisions and act independently. However, even in such moment, a human might seek at the bottom of their heart for someone who will support him. This novel depicts the process of the development of the protagonist's self. In this process she changes her companions and finally finds her eternal companion.

I have no one who supports me—. To Emily, her family is not an entity that supports her. Especially, her elder sister, two years older, irritates Emily's inferiority complex. Her sister is strong-willed, does well at school, and has decisive likes and dislikes. She is exactly the opposite of Emily. Emily is not a favorite in her family, but she has one talent. That is to make "stories." By and by, she develops her skill to entertain her friends by telling false stories. She inflates her stories at her listeners' requests, making her mother into a shoplifter at the store where she works and her father into someone suffering from loan-shark hell.

Everyone wants to be appreciated by the people around them. Normally, the family first makes them feel that they are precious and indispensable by words or in attitude. That sense of security leads them to meet someone else. But in the case of Emily, who has failed in impressing herself on her family, she repeatedly creates false stories to escape from the misery, and it is not long before she is called "Emily, the liar" and comes to be bullied by her classmates.

She looks for someone who will support her. First, it is a cat, Tom. It is a stray cat she began keeping when she was in a kindergarten. It looks cute at first, but as it grows bigger, it gets ugly, twisted and timid. The fact that the timid and unhappy cat appears more miserable than her gives Emily peace of mind. But when she is moved to a new home to escape from being bullied, she cannot keep the cat. Deprived from the mental support, Emily cannot adjust herself to the new environment and returns to be "Emily, the liar." Lies support Emily mentally in the days without the cat, allowing her to create a self-image freely and attracting people.

In her stories, "God" sometimes appears. It doesn't mean that she believes in God. She only develops her stories, following her imagination, and at the end she concludes her stories with such expressions as: "God knows everything." This might show that however far she escapes from the reality and sinks into the world of dreams, her sting of conscience from her telling lies makes her turn towards God.

Her mother is disappointed at Emily and approaches a strange religious sect for help. At last Emily is sent away from home and is moved into the sect's Cuckoo's Home in the countryside to "purify her soul." It is a nice way of abandoning a child.

The question that occurred first to my mind was what I would do if I had such a child, and I thought that what Emily needed most was a person who believed in and waited for growth of the child's self. However, who can expect that from actual parents? I suspect I would do as Emily's mother does.

Emily lives there from the summer through the winter. The life in the house for "problem children" teaches her to hate, betray and revenge, and fear for retribution. One night, she is locked up in a freezing cold barn. Feeling the threat of death, she escapes from the house like a jail.

I will escape from this place and survive—. A careful consideration leads to the realization that this is the first decision she has ever made. "A crucial moment," which I have referred to at the beginning of this essay, has come. She has been a child obedient enough to consent to her mother's instruction to move into Cuckoo's Home only from her sense of guilt. The weakness of the self urges us to obey people's suggestion against our own interests. This deed cannot be evaluated as being good-natured or compassionate. It means that the person's willpower is weak, and that the power to insist on what he or she wants to do, to be, or to refuse has not been cultivated. It might have arisen from her character, but it can be said that her mind has not yet developed as much as it should have. (Although the author makes the strange religious figure say that the protagonist was born too early without having accumulated good deeds, the readers might not understand it. The common feature between the two conceptions seems to be that their selves are immature.)

"The crucial moment" to Emily was the moment of awakening to the self. Before that, Emily, as if looking through semi-transparent glass, did not observe the outer world or other people. She had no will to live self-consciously. Her self, or her sense of self-identity, was too vulnerable. Although her sister is good at getting on in life, her mother is full of vanity, and her father is indifferent to raising children, they all might be normal people. Only Emily does not have normal quantity of self. Only to get rid of her sense of inferiority she regresses to her infancy and tries to live in the world of fiction. The fact that the contents of her stories are so antisocial as to disparage her family causes tragedy.

It can be said that every one of us spends the days looking through glass until a certain time, although Emily's glass seems to be much thicker than others'. It is a protective film against a severe reality until we recognize others and become strong enough to fight against the outer world, and as we grow up, it should melt or be torn by something or other. In Emily's case, it is forcibly torn by a severe environment. Although it might be possible to suppose what would have happened if she had not been sent to Cuckoo's Home, we cannot simply tell which was better. There ought to be due trials drawn by fate. One needs to experience the stages in one's rites of passage repeatedly in order to meet one's own self.

During the two days of her runaway journey, Emily struggles to survive, using all her skills, including telling lies. The lies are no longer buoyant or amusing, but they are told for her survival. She gets completely exhausted from telling lies. She thinks she would rather die than tell more lies. It is exactly a confrontation between Emily and a lie.

In such moment she meets and is fascinated by an old man when she is waiting for a night train, sitting on a bench at a station. There arises from him an air of sufferings he has long borne, resignation, endurance and gentleness. I think she superimposes God in her stories on the old man. She needs an existence by her side that waits patiently without irritation while a person takes a long time before waking up to the sins they have committed. This old man's image stays in her mind and continues to watch over her. Seeing an image of God in the old man, Emily drifts over the threshold between life and death.

The next day she meets a middle-aged man who was deprived of his beloved daughter by his wife in quarrel. (For some reasons, he reminds me of Emily's father.) He persuades her to die together. Emily struggles desperately to persuade him to refrain from suicide, when she feels that old man is inviting her to heaven. She tears herself away from the two, and escapes to the world of life.

Emily has escaped death. She spends Christmas in a hospital and goes back home. Although the danger of death has gone, she is desolate. Her mother and other family members appear uncomfortable. As Emily has suspected, her home does not seem to be a place for her. When she had decided to escape from Cuckoo's Home, the direction she had chosen was not to her home where her family lived, but to the opposite. She recollects the night: the snow field where she walked alone under heavy pressure of solitude and loneliness as if she were under the deep sea, and the daybreak and the heavenly light which almost erased the memory of the night. She felt God's blessing. She wonders what it meant. At that moment, for the first time, she could feel she was really alive.

She says to herself, "I must live on my own, and I must not bear a grudge or hatred against someone else. This way of living will fit well with me, even if it is hard." Then, a decision comes to her mind, "I will support myself after I graduate from junior high school." No one can expect this decision from what Emily once was. The gap between what she is and what she was is touching, but it might be necessary for her to sustain herself.

At night, her father mutters to her, "Was it cold then?" Emily laughs at the self-evident question. He then hands his name card to her, telling her to contact him when she is in trouble. The white card connects the two, a parent and a child as if it is the first time they meet. It sheds light just around her feet on the road ahead which is to be painful and severe to Emily, who has made up her mind to live alone.

This small offer of assistance bridges her mind with hope.

Hayao Kawai in *Kazoku Kankei o Kangaeru* [Contemplation on Family Relationship] refers to an expression, "an eternal companion." At a cultural seminar, Kawai said, "An eternal companion for an individual is not a finite particular person or a fragile object, but shapeless, everlasting, and universal values in his or her mind."

I would say that another name for "eternal companion" is "hope." Hope is mental energy which is essential for human beings to live. "Eternal companion" changes its faces, depending on each person. The faces are a creative activity for one person and a pursuit of truth or belief for another. An eternal companion stays close beside each person with a suitable face to every individual, encouraging him or her, helping them recover from a collapse and encouraging their self-realization.

And, Emily's eternal companion is God, who always watches over her.

This novel shows Christian influence. God, betrayal, retribution, the night near the winter solstice, blessing, heaven, resurrection, an encounter with the father, a promise—these motives are embedded in the various parts of the story. After reading this book, I learned that the author was born into a Christian family and her father had passed away recently. I was convinced of my supposition.

It is not clear whether the author believes Christianity or not, or whether she intended to adopt it as a basis of this work. However, I perceive in this too dark story a wide flow, that is, a prayer for the existence of God who watches over and always stands beside weak humans.

I realized that many classics in children's literature had mythology, religion or folklores as their backbone. Examples include: Ancient mythology, Kore-Cosmos (universal eye)[1], in *Momo* (1973) by Michael Ende, Christianity in *The Chronicles of Narnia* (1950–54) by C. S. Lewis, Welsh mythology, Mabinogion, that flows in *The Owl Service* (1967) by Alan Garner and northern folklores in *Chibikko Kamu no Boken* [Little Kam's Adventure] (1961) by a Japanese author, Toshiko Kanzawa.

The scale of stories created by individuals is enlarged dramatically when these streams flow into them. And when the contemporary authors' spirit proves its artistic worth in the great river of mythology and religion, their works will grasp the readers' heart. In that sense, I see such power in this novel.

Before the scene of the father and the child in the last chapter, the author has not given hope to the readers. Until then, my heart almost aches, wondering how the author will settle the gloomy and pent-up development.

However, a single name card overturns the sentiment. Here, the father and the child encounter. An encounter with Father (= God) in Christianity, who watches over the weak girl beside her as an eternal companion in the form of the real father's body, is depicted dramatically. This chapter filled me with great joy. For, I could perceive firm hope at the very end.

Note

1. *Kore-Cosmos*: an idea in *Hermetica* in the time of Hellenism (Akiyama 203).
   Kore: "daughter" or "eye" in Greek.
   Cosmos: "universe" in Greek.

Works Consulted

Akiyama, Satoko 秋山さと子. *Satori no Bunseki: Bukkyo to Yungu Shinrigaku to no Setten* [An Analysis of Enlightenment: Where Buddhism and Jungian Psychology Meet] 悟りの分析：仏教とユング心理学との接点. 1980. Tokyo: PHP Kenkyujo PHP研究所, 1991.

Kawai, Hayao 河合隼雄. *Kazoku Kankei o Kangaeru* [Contemplation on Family Relationship] 家族関係を考える. Tokyo: Kodansha 講談社, 1980.

Kudo, Sachio 工藤左千夫. *Fantaji Bungaku no Sekai e: Shukan no Tetsugaku no tame ni* [To the World of Fantasy: Philosophy of Subjectivity] ファンタジー文学の世界へ：主観の哲学のために. Tokyo: Seibunsha 成文社, 1992.

Shibamura, Kiyo 柴村紀代. *Usotsuki Emiri* [Emily, the Liar] うそつきエミリー. Tokyo: Dainippon Tosho 大日本図書, 1996.

Chapter III

What Mice Suggest to Us
—The Creatures That Dwell in Another World—

I recently went picking edible wild plants. It was an occasion for me to enjoy walking around the fields and hills. I found some trees which had had the bark at their foot peeled off. My uncle, who accompanied me, told me that it was done by field mice. Afterward, I learned from a book that mice did it to take in water. The book is *Nezumi ni Osowareru Toshi* [Cities Attacked by Rats] by Tatsuo Yabe. It reports the damages caused by mice and that they are still active in the present day. When I was young, house cats still caught mice, but for children today, mice might be animals that exist only in stories. According to the book, however, the territory for modern mice's activity has only shifted from households to big buildings in cities and the damages are huge. Mice appear to have a great effect on humans even today.

While I reflected upon these, a thought came to my mind that many of my favorite children's books I had been reading featured mice, or rather, not only in my favorite books but also in children's books in general mice are important characters.

Why must it be a mouse? When an author of children's books chooses a mouse from among many kinds of animals as a character or thinks it must be a mouse, not any other animal, he or she might want a mouse to express something within themselves, and mice themselves, too, seem to have something to tell us. I would like to try to search for the answer in the six works chosen from the books I have read.

#1—The Discovery of the Free World: *The Mousewife* (Fairy Tale)

Rumer Godden
The Mousewife
Illustrated by William P. du Bois
London: Macmillan, 1951

* Japanese edition: Godden, Rumer. *Nezumi Nyobo*. Trans. Momoko Ishii. Tokyo: Fukuinkan Shoten, 1977.

The protagonist is a young female mouse who is pregnant. The author, Godden, entrusts the mouse with her dreams and hopes. The author is forty-four years old, and having got over the busiest part of bringing her children, she is at the period of looking back over her life and asks herself, "Can I approve of my way of life, or shouldn't I have lived another life?" At one time or another, a feeling of emptiness that the life has been filled only with daily tasks to be done assails a middle-aged woman. So, the author provided the protagonist, a young female mouse, with a chance to discover for the author what the author herself could not have seen.

In the house where the mousewife lives, a wild dove is kept in a cage. The mousewife goes near to the cage because she wants to eat the peas there. And through the conversations with the dove, a visitor from the wide open sky, as it were, a free world, she discovers that the stars seen at night over the windowsill are not brass buttons, but they are real and shining very far off. That is to say, the mousewife, who is much younger than the author, discovers that outside the world in which she lives (= in the house) there exists another world. This discovery does seem to me a great step for women in general, rather than the personal regret or the desire of the author herself. The mouse, now, stands at the door open to the new world.

#2—The Recognition of the World of Hope: *Frederick* (Picture Book)

Leo Lionni
Frederick
New York: Knopf, 1967

* Japanese edition: Lionni, Leo. *Furederikku*. Trans. Shuntaro Tanikawa. Tokyo: Kogakusha, 1969.

Next comes a male wild mouse. While the others are busy preparing for the winter, Frederic appreciates "time" absent-mindedly. At the end of the winter, all their food is eaten up. When the others are losing hope, he begins to talk of the warm sunlight, beautiful flowers and busy insects that will surely come back. In his heart, "time" has been changed into poetry. When they shut their eyes, a clear picture of a world of hope appears before them. They survive by recognizing the time of hope in their mind.

#3—The Compensation for the Dark World Hidden in the Mind: *The Pied Piper of Hamelin* (Picture Book, an Illustration of a Historical Fact in Germany in 1284)

Poems by Robert Browning
The Pied Piper of Hamelin
Illustrated by Kate Greenaway

London: Frederick Warne, 1888

* Japanese edition: Browning, Robert. *Hamerun no Fuefuki*. Trans. Sumiko Yagawa. Tokyo: Bunka Shuppankyoku, 1976.

Whereas the mice mentioned in the preceding works break out the impasse by attaining another world, the mice featured in this story are harmful and to be eliminated by humans. The city, Hamelin, which is troubled by a plague of mice, asks a piper with a magical power to exterminate them. After the piper has accomplished the mission, a greedy mayor and others refuse to pay a reward for it. The piper gets angry and he takes all the children of the city with him to a secret place. What has been lost are the community's children, who are the hope and the future of the city. We sometimes try to exterminate what is unfavorable for us with the power of money, and by ignoring our conscience we try not to see it. However, to see whole thing means to accept both the favorable and the unfavorable for us. To refuse to see the shadow in our mind takes unexpected compensation.

#4—To the Unknown World: *The Adventurers* **(Children's Literature)**

Atsuo Saito
Bokenshatachi **[The Adventurers]**
Tokyo: Arisukan Bokushinsha, 1972

Whenever I look at my sons' selection of books, the titles with "ogres" or "adventures" seem to attract more of their interest than the titles with "heart." According to my observation, what an adventure means differs depending on the sex. It might be my bias, but I would claim that, generally speaking, women tend to attach importance to the internal (mental) adventure such as change in attitude in *The Mousewife*, whereas men tend to seek for external adventure, such as the fight against the unknown world or enemies. In this sense, this story might be a manly adventure story. The protagonist, a young male mouse, Gamba, goes to a party on the boat with his friends for a change. They meet with boat mice by chance and go with them to an island which is ruled by weasels, mice's natural enemies. What they win after the deadly fight is love, courage and friendship. Involved in the story, we live another self, given amazing ability, courage or chance which we could never attain in the real world. Adventures unfolded in the story refresh our spirit and provoke the unknown potential in the readers and the courage to challenge it.

#5—The Last Phase of a Dream: *Flowers for Algernon* **(Young Adult Literature)**

Daniel Keyes
Flowers for Algernon
New York: Harcourt Brace, 1966
* Japanese edition: Keyes, Daniel. *Arujanon ni Hanataba o*. Trans. Fusa Obi. Tokyo: Hayakawa Shobo, 1978.

Charlie Gordon is thirty-two years old. His IQ is raised from 68 to 185 by the power of science, that is, brain surgery. What makes him decide it is his desire to be loved by his mother. He is slow at learning and he thinks that his mother will love him if he becomes clever. However, he cannot win love even after he becomes a genius. And then, an unexpected rapid decline of his intelligence occurs. His intelligence gets lower than before the surgery. He learns his end from a white mouse, Algernon, who took the same surgery before him. Charlie has no time. He is nearing his end. Now he has the smartest brain in the world, and being conscious of the desperate deterioration, he publishes excellent research findings which contribute to human beings. The high intelligence, which is a human dream, doesn't last. Not only he, but also we, all have a deep-rooted blind belief that a bright child is considered to be a good child who is to be loved. Many people do not value what they are and believe that they should improve themselves. Thus, what makes humans long for a high intelligence? I vaguely suspect that we need it in order to survive. The world Charlie dreamed of might be another world each of us wishes to gain.

The biggest differences between a human and a mouse, apart from intelligence, might be the size of the body and the life span. According to *Zo no Jikan Nezumi no Jikan* [The Elephant's Time and the Mouse's Time], written by a biologist, Tatsuo Motokawa, while the elephant lives for sixty to one hundred years, the mouse lives for only half of the elephant's life span. In spite of the fact, the number of breaths and the beating of the heart in their lifetime is the same. It can be said that the shortness of the life span is counterbalanced by its intensity. That is to say, Charlie had to live a mouse's life although he was a human. And the impetuous desire to attain a dream might have changed a human into a mouse.

#6—The Road to Coexistence: *The Class Schedule after School* (Children's Literature)

Jun Okada
Hokago no Jikanwari [The Class Schedule after School]
Tokyo: Kaiseisha, 1980

Science has brought us invaluable comfort to our daily life. On the other hand, the terrific speed of progress often cherishes an illusion in us that progress is connected straight to happiness. However, we also have cultural properties we have matured without haste, including mythologies, folklores and legends peculiar to each ethnic group. They have kept changing with the times. What I will deal with last is "the new mice" that have their own stories. In this story, the human and the mouse are on equal footing.

One day, a young art teacher rescues a mouse from a cat. To his surprise, the mouse wears a white gown and eye-glasses. He is one of the school-mice who live in the school. They were called a first-year-student mouse, a school-ground mouse, a night-guard's-room mouse, and etc. depending on where they lived. The mouse says they had a lot of magnificent stories. However, the art-room mouse, who is the only survivor, resolves to approach a human, for he realized that if he died before telling their stories to someone, their fruitful culture would vanish. Mice live very close to humans, almost in the same space, just behind the ceiling-boards, the wall-boards, or the floor boards. This school mouse has developed his intelligence by listening to humans' lessons and has formed cultural properties peculiar to them. He is an evolved mouse. The teacher begins to listen to the mouse's stories attentively. How interesting, gorgeous and mysterious they are! The two spend a pleasant time together once a week. After a while, the time for parting draws near. The teacher is leaving for a new school. He suggests the mouse to move to the new school with him, but the mouse refuses. Thus, the teacher, who has now inherited the culture of the school mouse, settles at the art room of the new school. He calls out toward the ceiling, "Hey. You school-mice of this school, if you can hear me, please respond to me." Then, there comes a sound, *Knock*. This story ends, suggesting that there is another group of school mice. Humans are able to listen to their stories and pass them on to others. We are not the world's greatest authority. From now on, the world where we can live alongside the school mice is waiting for us. What this means is very significant.

In the first five stories discussed above, the mice move around in the dark, but in #6, the mouse comes out for the first time into the place under the light. In trying to trace the transition I find that "mice" might be our other selves that dwell in our unconscious.

When humans confront sincerely their other selves in their mind (*The Mousewife*), without refusing to see the negative aspect (*The Pied Piper of Hamelin*), and step out to the new world bravely (*The Adventurers*), they will find the light full of hope (*Frederick*). However, if they try to widen their dominion too impetuously, the door to the new world will be sometimes closed

(*Flowers for Algernon*). Only in the leisurely process of fostering the stories, the culture of their own, the road toward the encounter and the coexistence with another valuable and flourishing culture will be cut open (*The Class Schedule after School*).

That is, the transition of the mice from #1 to #6 shows the process of the unconscious in the deep layer in our mind being made conscious gradually. Now, what is the benefit of making the unconscious conscious?

The trigger which made me interested in the unconscious was a children's story, *Nemuriya-san* [A Sleep Inn], by Sukeyuki Imanishi. A mother and a son have run away from home and they are going to stay a night on the bench at a train station. An inn-keeper appears and offers them a stay at his inn. The charge is to tell him about the dream they have dreamed that night. The mother, perplexed, tells him about her hope that her little son succeeds in life, changing it into her dream. Her son says honestly that he had a dream in which he ate with his father. The mother is at a loss for words and the inn-keeper, discovering what the child's hope is, urges the two to go home.

Our unconscious most easily perceived is our dream in our sleep. Unexpected contents in our mind sometimes pop up in our dreams. Humans do not necessarily know all that is in their mind. It seems that our other selves dwell in the subliminal world. By making the unconscious conscious, we can encounter our other selves.

What are we humans seeking for? Let me suggest that we are seeking for the way to live which we are satisfied with. Is it possible to gain it in this way? Am I not proceeding in the wrong direction? We, being confronted with these countless choices, might approach step by step to the answer by looking at the depth of our mind.

Mice are small and very cautious. They live in the dark and form what to us appears a chaotic troop and we do not know what they are doing. And, they are sometimes used for good contributing to mankind as pets or laboratory animals, and sometimes do harm as carriers of germs or by damaging our crops. Moreover, the mice are parasitic only on humans. That is to say, mice are very close to us humans. In spite of the fact, we have little knowledge of them. In other words, we do not bother ourselves knowing them. Isn't this relationship similar to that between us and our unconscious? We might be scared to look into it in the depth of our mind. Even if it really exists, we do not know how to face it, so that we ignore it as if it does not exist.

However, the unconscious is not a mouse that does only harm. It conveys to us marvelously rich and attractive stories and messages as the school mouse does. The world where mice dwell is just behind the thin boards. When humans search how to live, inspired by mice, these small creatures will unfold another world, the unconscious, before us.

Works Consulted

Abe, Kin'ya 阿部謹也. *Hamerun no Fuefuki Otoko* [The Pied Piper of Hamelin] ハーメルンの笛吹き男. 1974. Tokyo: Chikuma Shobo 筑摩書房, 1988.

Browning, Robert. *Hamerun no Fuefuki* [The Pied Piper of Hamelin] ハメルンの笛吹き. Trans. Yagawa Sumiko 矢川澄子. Tokyo: Bunka Shuppankyoku 文化出版局, 1976.

---. *The Pied Piper of Hamelin*. London: Frederick Warne, 1888.

Ende, Michael. *Hamerun no Shi no Buto* ハーメルンの死の舞踏. Trans. Sato Mariko 佐藤真理子, and Koyasu Michiko 子安美知子. Tokyo: Asahi Shinbunsha 朝日新聞社, 1993. Trans. of *Der Rattenfänger: Ein Hamelner Totentanz*. Stuttgart: Weitbrecht, 1993.

Godden, Rumer. *The Mousewife*. 1951. *Mouse Time: Two Stories*. London: Pan Macmillan, 1993. 8-29.

---. *Nezumi Nyobo* [The Mousewife] ねずみ女房. Trans. Ishii Momoko 石井桃子. Tokyo: Fukuinkan Shoten 福音館書店, 1977.

Imanishi, Sukeyuki 今西祐行. *Nemuriya-san* [A Sleep Inn] ねむり屋さん. Tokyo: Asunaro Shobo あすなろ書房, 1985.

Kawai, Hayao 河合隼雄. *Konpurekkusu* [Complex] コンプレックス. Tokyo: Iwanami Shoten 岩波書店, 1971.

---. *Muishiki no Kozo* [Structure of Unconsciousness] 無意識の構造. Tokyo: Chuo Koronsha 中央公論社, 1977.

Keyes, Daniel. *Arujanon ni Hanataba o* [Flowers for Algernon] アルジャーノンに花束を. Trans. Obi Fusa 小尾芙佐. Tokyo: Hayakawa Shobo 早川書房, 1978.

---. *Flowers for Algernon*. New York: Harcourt Brace, 1966.

Lionni, Leo. *Frederick*. New York: Knopf, 1967.

---. *Furederikku* [Frederick] フレデリック. Trans. Tanikawa Shuntaro 谷川俊太郎. Tokyo: Kogakusha 好学社, 1969.

Motokawa, Tatsuo 本川達雄. *Zo no Jikan Nezumi no Jikan* [The Elephant's Time and the Mouse's Time] ゾウの時間ネズミの時間. Tokyo: Chuo Koronsha 中央公論社, 1992.

Okada, Jun 岡田淳. *Hokago no Jikanwari* [The Class Schedule after School] 放課後の時間割. Tokyo: Kaiseisha 偕成社, 1980.

Saito, Atsuo 斎藤惇夫. *Bokenshatachi* [The Adventurers] 冒険者たち. Tokyo: Arisukan Bokushinsha アリス館牧新社, 1972.

Yabe, Tatsuo 矢部辰男. *Nezumi ni Osowareru Toshi* [Cities Attacked by Rats] ネズミに襲われる都市. Tokyo: Chuo Koronsha 中央公論社, 1998.

Chapter IV

Imagination and Freedom
—Ability the Mousewife Acquired—

" . . . and she knew, all at once, that was where the dove should be, in the trees and the garden and the wood."

—Rumer Godden, *The Mousewife*

Rumer Godden
The Mousewife

Illustrated by William P. du Bois

London: Macmillan, 1951

* Japanese edition: Godden, Rumer. *Nezumi Nyobo*. Trans. Momoko Ishii. Tokyo: Fukuinkan Shoten, 1977.

About fifteen years ago, I met with the fable[1], *The Mousewife*, and was fascinated by it. First, I did not know why, but while I repeated reading it, the mouse protagonist settled in my heart. The longer I lived with her, the more I liked her. It led me to desire to clarify what the mouse and the story intended to covey to us.

First, I will summarize the story.

*   *   *

There lives a female mouse in a house. She looks the same as other mice, and she wants something but doesn't know what it is. One day, a wild male dove is brought into the house to be kept. The dove, deprived of freedom, refused to eat anything. The mouse approaches him, attracted by the food in the cage, and soon they begin to talk. She is charmed by the stories told by the dove of the sky and the smell of winds and soil. She frequently goes to the windowsill by the dove and the male mouse complains about that. After a while the mouse delivers her babies and she gets too busy to visit the dove. When she goes to the dove after a long time, she finds the dove dying. She decides to set the dove free and she succeeds, helped by the luck that the window is left open.

The dove flies away, and, she feels sorry that she will not be able to listen to the dove's stories any more, when she sees the stars in the night sky and realizes that she is looking at them with her own eyes. Long after that, she is now a great-great-grand mother, and is respected and thought highly of by the mice around her.

*   *   *

The author of this story is Rumer Godden, a British writer. It was written more than fifty years ago, and the Japanese translation I have is by Momoko Ishii. It was published thirty-six years ago and has been repeatedly reissued.

Recently, I found that there was another translation by another translator. I tried comparing the two translations, looking at the original text and found remarkable differences. I remembered Masako Shimizu's words referring to translation. Masako Shimizu is the translator of *Earthsea* fantasy series (1968–2001), an American children's literature, by Ursula K. Le Guin, and a critic of children's literature.

She says that the translators' conception of children is related to their translation of children's books. She might mean that their way of life emerges in their translation (121). Many of children's books are from overseas. Therefore, the influence of the translators is immense.

I will refer to the details of the three books.

The original text:
The Mousewife (London: Macmillan, 1951)
Story by Rumer Godden (UK)
Illustrated by William P. du Bois (USA)

Japanese editions:
#1—*Nezumi no Okamisan* ネズミの おかみさん (Tokyo: Kaiseisha, 1965)
Translated by Keiko Kuriyagawa
Illustrated by Keiko Akana

#2—*Nezumi Nyobo* ねずみ女房 (Tokyo: Fukuinkan Shoten, 1977)
Translated by Momoko Ishii
Illustrated by William P. du Bois

TRANSLATOR'S PROFILES

Keiko Kuriyagawa (1924–)
Place of Birth: Hoten, Manchuria.
Education: English Department, Keio University.
Translations: *Tales from Shakespeare* by C. Lamb and M. Lamb, *Peter Pan* by J. M. Barrie.

Momoko Ishii (1907–2008)
Place of Birth: Saitama prefecture.
Education: English Department, Japan Women's University.
A Writer of Children's Literature.
Writings: *Non-chan Kumo ni Noru* [Non-chan on the Clouds], *Sangatsu*

Hina no Tsuki [March, the Month of Hina-dolls], *Osana Monogatari* [Story of the Young].

Translations: *The Wind in the Willows* by Kenneth Grahame, *Winnie the Pooh* by A. A. Milne, the *Peter Rabbit* series by Beatrix Potter.

I will observe the difference between the two translations.

Illustrations: The mouse is naked in the original and the translation #2, and is dressed like a human in the translation #1.

Headings: In the translation #1, there are three subheadings, which the original does not have.

Afterword: The translation #1 does not have the afterword written by the author of the original. Instead, it has its translator's comments.

These findings show that the translation #1 altered the original, whereas the translation #2 is faithful to the original.

The title of the translation #1 is *Nezumi no Okamisan*, and that of the translation #2 is *Nezumi Nyobo*. The original title is *The Mousewife*. The difference comes from the selection of the words.

As a matter of course, the stories are the same in the translations #1 and #2, but the words chosen are different in many places. This might be caused by the translators' concept of children or children's books, as is mentioned by Shimizu. Moreover, there is a gap of twelve years between the times when the two were translated, and the historical background and the intention of the publishers might have influenced the making of the two.

I once talked with Ishii on the phone to ask her how to acquire the original text, and I found that she did not know that Kuriyagawa's translation existed. That means that Ishii was not influenced by or considered Kuriyagawa's translation.

The publisher's intention might have influenced the translation #1. The concept of the publishers differs greatly between the translation #1 and #2. The translation #1 aimed at only children and put cute cloths on the animals to please children, added subheadings to make the book easy to read for children and deleted Godden's afterword. The translator suggested in her afterword that the theme of this story was the friendship between "the mousewife and the dove" (Kuriyagawa, "Hori to Aibi" 159), but I do not agree.

On the other hand, Ishii did not write an afterword or comments. Godden's afterward is not deleted. Her translation is straight and faithful. In translation #1, the scene where the dove kisses the mouse is not translated. It might be the consideration to the young readers. Although many of the readers of the translation #2, including me, might ask if this is really a children's book, the translation #1 will not raise this question. I think this book is written for both children and adults, and so might Ishii have thought. Ishii said that children's literature should "interest both children and adults" ("The Significance of Realism" 140).

She respected children and children's books, and wrote, "I have never despised children and I always appreciate the works done by the people with deep affection for children" ("Stray Thoughts on Children's Literature").

Here, I will look at Rumer Godden. She was born in Sussex, UK in 1907. She lived in India from the age of several months to thirteen and went back to England. She wrote *The Doll's House* (1947) at the age of forty. After that, she devoted herself to writing. She wrote many stories featuring small things and animals. Also she wrote stories for adults, poems and dramas. She died in 1998. Her books for children include *The Kitchen Madonna* (1967), *The Diddakoi* (1972) and *Little Plum* (1963).

She was born in the same year as Ishii, and her works are being translated into Japanese even now. I called this work "fable" at the beginning of this essay. I quoted this expression from a criticism and introduction of British children's literature, *Igirisu Jido Bungaku no Sakkatachi: Fantaji to Riarizumu* [The British Writers of Children's Literature—Fantasy and Realism] by Yoko Inokuma and Teruo Jingu. In this book, Inokuma writes that Godden ardently admired Andersen and she wrote his biography and that she was "a black sheep" in her family just as Andersen was "an ugly duckling" (101).

According to Inokuma, Godden, who was inferior to her elder sister in many respects, knew absurdity of life, and drew a miniature world of dolls that was full of the delights and the sorrows, beauty and ugliness in life (101-04). (The same might be true of her depiction of the world of many small animals.) Inokuma concludes her essay by saying, "that is why Godden's works are not only fables but also the works that both children and adults can appreciate, reflecting their own experiences" (104).

H. C. Andersen said to one of his friends, Ingemann[2], as is referred to by Shizuka Yamamuro in his biography of Andersen, "Now I stare into myself for ideas appealing to the older people, and write about them as if I were telling the stories to children, keeping it in mind that their parents are also listening to them" (168).

This attitude is shared with Godden. In the translation #1, the voice of the narrator is not heard. This is partly because the author's afterword is deleted. In the translation #2, the voice of the narrator is heard in some places, in the expressions, "I think . . . ," as is heard in the original. This "I" is the author, and the voice of the author leads to the afterword.

Ishii grasps this attitude of Godden's toward children and children's books. That is clear in the Japanese equivalents to the title. The Japanese word, "okamisan," in the translation #1 is different in nuance from "nyobo" in the translation #2. I consulted *Kojien*, a Japanese dictionary, for these words.

* "Okami": somebody's wife; a female cook; a proprietress of an inn.
* "Okamisan": an honorific of a proprietress.
* "Nyobo": [1] a court-lady's room. [2] a high-ranked court-lady given a room of her own. [3] a married woman, wife, a lady.
* "Bo": [1] a room, a chamber of a court-lady. [2] a shape divided into many rooms.

Many of Japanese folktales have titles with "nyobo," including *Tsuru-nyobo* [Crane-wife], *Esugata-nyobo* [Portrait-wife] and *Tennin-nyobo* [Celestial-nymph-wife]. However, I cannot remember the titles with "okamisan."

Both "okamisan" and "nyobo" are a little old-fashioned, but "okamisan" is more common than "nyobo." "Okamisan" has an image that she is cheerful, good-natured and hard working. "Nyobo" is a strong-willed and expressive woman. It has an impression that she lives in a smaller room, self-restraining and lonesome. I can see two patterns in "nyobo" in the translation #2.

(a) Positive woman: a woman with great discernment who has her own free space (a room, a world).

(b) Negative woman: a detained woman locked up in a small room given to her.

This reminds me of *A Room of One's Own* (1929) by Virginia Woolf (1882–1941). In this book, she claims that women should have a room of their own. She is one of the forerunners of British feminist writers and critics. She committed suicide by jumping into water at the age of fifty-nine. It was ten years before Godden wrote *The Mousewife*. The difference of the titles between Kuriyagawa's and Ishii's shows to what degrees they discern the essence of the story. This mouse is not a softhearted housewife. I support Ishii's choice of the word, "nyobo."

This story can be read as a narrative of the process of the growth of a woman from being a negative woman into a positive one, for the mouse first did not know what she wanted, but she turned into a being that had her own world.

This mouse seems to be a little peculiar, but, to me, she seems to be a part of myself. I might have been one of the women who lacked nothing particular but wanted something of her own, different from others'. I encountered this book when I was a mother insensible to this sense of being myself. I felt with a flash of intuition that this book had something significant to me, and borrowed it repeatedly from the library. I also recommended it to my neighbors and friends.

This book had the power to urge me to do that. It made me desire to be connected with others by sharing it. I wanted to ask the lady who lived next door, "Haven't you thought like this?" In fact, I asked many people these questions. The main point of it was about the relationship between the dove and the female mouse and what the mouse wanted. The people I shared the book with reacted differently on these questions and on other points:

A teenage junior-high girl: I felt pity for the dove. The people who captured the dove in the cage are wrong. The dove must be free. The relation between the dove and the mouse is spiritual.

A teenage high school boy: Some may think the relation as adultery, but what's wrong if you commit "adultery in the mind"?

A woman in her twenties: This protagonist has no reason. She takes revenge on her husband by being respected by her grandchildren when she has got old. I am angry that the male mouse's action is exactly the same as the human male.

A woman in her twenties: The scene where the male mouse bite the female mouse was painful.

A woman in her thirties: Having written down on the paper the lyrics to the first verse of *Ihojin* [A Stranger] by Saki Kubota, she said, "This song expresses how the female mouse feels."

I will explain the reason she remembered this song. I found from a TV show that *A Stranger* was very popular among middle-aged women who sang at karaoke bars. I myself, a middle-aged woman, love it very much. I was pleased to know that there were people who shared my love for this song, and thought that they also shared what I felt in it. I love it because of the vast expanse of the scene and the unknown world which stirs my heart. The song is about a sentiment of a woman who has parted from a lover and has set off on a sentimental journey. However, the situation disappears from the listeners, and the feeling of their closed heart being unfolded and becoming free spreads pleasantly. Presumably, the image of the new space of the foreign land makes those effects. I told her this impression of mine, and, as a result, she made her comments I have mentioned.

A housewife in her thirties: Is this a book for children? It is like scandals in newspapers, but I think it isn't. Is it calming to know what we have not known?

A woman in her forties: Although I first thought this story to be about a woman who wants to leap over a boundary of common-sense or about adultery, I later thought the female mouse might represent women who were not satisfied with their existing circumstances and wonder if there was something else. However, this mouse returns to the real life and is satisfied with it. This attitude seems to be a compromise.

A woman in her forties: Isn't it a story of a love affair?

A woman in her fifties: I can hear the sigh of a housewife who lives with a husband who throws his weight about.

A woman in her fifties: This male mouse ties the female mouse, who is out of touch with reality, to the real life. He is an important character.

A woman in her seventies: What is it? Is it a book for children?

In summarizing the reactions of the readers, I found the difference in the degree of the tolerance for freedom. The younger the readers were, the more tolerant they were. The younger readers thought that to have tender sentiments is not something to be ashamed about. The older people tended to regard it as a taboo. The women in their thirties longed for freedom, and they didn't seem to regard the connotation of immorality in the relationships between the dove and the female mouse as a problem. It might be caused by their ethical viewpoint much freer than that of the women in their seventies. Compared to the women in their thirties, they might not have experienced the freedom of romance and have a sense of taboo for romance or love affairs as well as a longing for it. The women in-between, in their forties and fifties, might be a wavering generation. A half of them thought that what was expressed by the female mouse to be a longing for a love affair or a housewife's grief, and the other half thought it to be more spiritual.

I am in the forties. First, I unquestioningly believed that it was about the female mouse's spirit. I was irritated with the people who thought that it was a song in praise of love or a love affair. I was resentful of the view that most housewives were frustrated, being shut off from the relationship with men and the society. The readers tended to give their attention to the relation between the female mouse and the dove, rather than to the ability to discern things, in which I was most interested. I desperately wanted to clarify what ability this mousewife had gained. After a while, I realized that it would be my bias to exclude the element of love from this story. Although Godden's main aim might not have been to depict the mouse's love for the dove, it would be impossible for her to perceive her own ability without it. In sharing this story with many people, my stiffness was gradually eased. People often bind themselves.

Then, one direction was in sight. The process toward the direction stretched from a confinement of a woman as an individual toward that of women in general, and, over the difference between the sexes, toward the issue of freedom of a human.

The readers might have realized the ability the mousewife had gained. They just could not make comments on it because it was too obscure to name and describe.

I was convinced that this female mouse became freer and freer. I thought what she needed in order to gain freedom was the ability to discern things.

In the middle of the story, there is an expression, "She looked far away"

(Godden 20), in the scene where her husband complains about his wife frequently going to the windowsill. She looks far away, saying nothing.

At this moment, for the first time, she might have realized that she was not free but in captivity. In the direction toward which she looked in seeking for her relief, she saw freedom. She might not have assented to her husband's complaints, and wondered why she should be blamed? At this moment, she might have begun to nurture the ability to see things only with her own eyes, that is, imagination. I believe that what she gained was the ability to imagine, which would take her to a free world.

If people see things without imagination, they will hardly know what it really is. This is clearly shown in the appearance of the female mouse looking out of the window vacantly. However, she had a young bud of the ability to imagine, and the stories told by the dove, who was an intruder from a free world, fostered it. The dove told of the boundless sky, of how it blew in the grass and the trees, of the scent of the damp soil, and of the dew drops on the leaves of the grass. All these were in the space unfamiliar to her and in the unknown world.

The dove continues to tell of his own world to support his own life. When it is interrupted by the female mouse's busy days, the dove's energy is almost exhausted. The female mouse, whose imagination was growing well enough to feel a dove's despair as a prisoner as if it were her own despair, let the dove free. The action was also to release her into a world of free way of thinking. However, she was not aware of it then, but, it was a moment later that she sensed it. So, she experienced a hard sense of loss when the dove flew away without looking back or expressing thanks to her. "He has flown. . . . Now there is no one to tell me about the hills and the corns and the clouds. I shall forget them" (26).

However, it was unnecessary to worry about it. The free world which she thought she would acquire only by being given did not vanish but continued to exist there. She looked up at the night sky with tears in her eyes, and she perceived her ability. She was able to see that the stars were very far off and shining.

This scene of almost simultaneous loss and gain is dynamic. I was deeply moved by the scene. However, first I could not explain clearly to myself the reason and what power moved me. Then I thought mice were a symbol of human's constrained psyche, and the mousewife is standing at the door of the world. And at last I reached the answer. The power is "imagination."

Godden says in her afterword that the idea of this story comes from the diary by Dorothy Wordsworth, the younger sister of Wordsworth, a poet. She goes on to say that although Dorothy did not let the dove out of the cage, she wanted strongly her mouse to set the dove free (Godden 29).

The author called the mouse "my mouse." It is natural to call her so because she is the heroine the author created. However, if each person has a mouse dwelling in their mind, they can manipulate it as they wish. So, here Godden might have meant to emphasize that the mouse was hers, not anyone else's. Godden's mouse released the captured dove, and at the same time, gained freedom within her.

Many of Godden's works have the same pattern. The protagonists have trouble with maladjustment to their environment, and then some incident or encounter occurs. The protagonists are distressed and with their own wisdom and strength they carve out their own future. They are dolls that are passive, a person who has no comfortable place for themselves, a discriminated person or the captured. However, they all rescue themselves. Godden might want to convey that humans have that potential by nature. Godden also saved herself by her imagination.

Since she was a child, she had liked poetry and outdoor activities (Kuriyagawa, "Hori to Aibi" 159). It is said that she was inferior in every aspect to her sisters, beautiful and talented. The only thing in which Godden was superior to her sisters was the ability to create stories. It is said that Godden did not fail to make stories whenever her sister, Joan, asked her to (Inokuma and Jingu 101-02). That is to say, the free space that the mouse had been searching for only for herself was, to Godden, creating stories.

That was the ability necessary for Godden to survive. This is similar to the dove's story-telling for survival. Story-telling liberated Godden from her inferiority complex and bitter circumstances. It is said that Godden was nostalgic for the life in India where she had lived until the age of thirteen and that she suffered from the life in England (qtd. in Inokuma and Jingu 100).

Sukeyuki Imanishi, a writer of children's literature, says that the bliss of reading stories is to see and hear what cannot be seen or heard in the real life. The source that gives the readers this bliss might be imagination. Imagination is indispensable for a writer.

Godden's experience is symbolized by the mouse and the dove. The author rescued herself, who is both the mouse and the dove. The outstanding symbolism not only tells the story of the strange mouse and the dove, but also works on the readers' emotions. The readers' imagination might be stimulated as well. This story has a power to enrich the readers' heart and leads us to contemplate even now, half a century after it was published. I myself feel that my imagination has been nurtured by this work.

What is freedom? It is what everyone wishes for from the bottom of their heart.

It is impossible to be one hundred percent free, but people are inclined not to notice that they are bound. It is only when we touch freedom or bump into a wall that we notice we are not free. I strongly believe that people should pursue their own way of life over the lifetime.

This story of *The Mousewife* suggests that freedom is expanded by cultivating the imagination with which people are endowed as it can lead to a completion of their inherent individuality.

Notes

1. Fable: "A short story, conveying a moral or irony, typically with animals as characters. They are symbols of humans, but retain the appearance and the features as animals" ("Guwa").
2. Bernhard Severin Ingemann (1789–1862): A Danish writer of historical

novels and a poet ("Bernhard").

Works Consulted

"Bernhard Severin Ingemann." *Wikipedia.* 20 Jan. 2016 <https://en.wikipedia.org/wiki/Bernhard_Severin_Ingemann>.

"Bo" 房. Shinmura.

"Guwa" [fable] 寓話. *Maipedia* [My Pedia] マイペディア. Tokyo: Heibonsha 平凡社, 1994.

Godden, Rumer. *The Mousewife.* 1951. *Mouse Time: Two Stories.* London: Pan Macmillan, 1993. 8-29.

Inokuma, Yoko 猪熊葉子, and Jingu Teruo 神宮輝夫. *Igirisu Jido Bungaku no Sakkatachi: Fantaji to Riarizumu* [The British Writers of Children's Literature—Fantasy and Realism] イギリス児童文学の作家たち：ファンタジーとリアリズム. Tokyo: Kenkyusha Shuppan 研究社出版, 1975.

Ishii, Momoko 石井桃子. "Jido Bungaku Zakkan" [Stray Thoughts on Children's Literature] 児童文学雑感. *Dokusho Shunju* [Reading Years] 読書春秋 Feb. 1952: 8-9.

---, trans. *Nezumi Nyobo* [The Mousewife] ねずみ女房. By Rumer Godden. Tokyo: Fukuinkan Shoten 福音館書店, 1977.

---. "Riarizumu no Taisetsusa" [The Significance of Realism] リアリズムの大切さ. *Dokushojin* [Readers] 読書人 8 Mar. 1965. Rpt. in *Esseishu* [Essays] エッセイ集. 138-40. Vol. 5 of *Ishii Momoko Korekushon* [The Collected Works of Momoko Ishii] 石井桃子コレクション. Tokyo: Iwanami Shoten 岩波書店, 2015.

Kubota, Saki 久保田早紀. *Ihojin* [A Stranger] 異邦人. CBS Sony, 1979.

Kuriyagawa, Keiko 厨川圭子. "Hori to Aibi no Monogatari ni tsuite" [About *The Story of Holly and Ivy*] ホリーとアイビーの物語について. Commentary. *Hori to Aibi no Monogatari* [The Story of Holly and Ivy] ホリーとアイビーの物語. By Rumer Godden. Trans. Kuriyagawa. Tokyo: Kaiseisha 偕成社, 1965. 158-60.

---, trans. "Nezumi no Okamisan" [The Mousewife] ネズミの　おかみさん. *Hori to*

Aibi no Monogatari [The Story of Holly and Ivy] ホリーとアイビーの物語. By Rumer Godden. Tokyo: Kaiseisha 偕成社, 1965. 127-57.

"Nyobo" 女房. Shinmura.

"Okami" おかみ. Shinmura.

"Okamisan" おかみさん. Shinmura.

Shimizu, Masako 清水眞砂子. *Kofuku ni Odoroku Chikara* [The Ability to Wonder at Happiness] 幸福に驚く力. Kyoto: Kamogawa Shuppan かもがわ出版, 2006.

Shinmura, Izuru 新村出, ed. *Kojien* [Japanese Dictionary] 広辞苑. 4th ed. Tokyo: Iwanami Shoten 岩波書店, 1991.

Woolf, Virginia. *A Room of One's Own*. London: Hogarth Press, 1929.

Yamamuro, Shizuka 山室静. *Andersen no Shogai* [The Biography of Andersen] アンデルセンの生涯. Tokyo: Shinchosha 新潮社, 1975.

Chapter V

From Being a Benefactor to Being a Friend
—The Cat Visitor—

Ruth Ainsworth
The Cat Visitor

London: Deutsch, 1963

* Japanese edition: Ainsworth, Ruth. *Kuroneko no Okyakusama*. Trans. Konomi Ara. Illus. Fujie, Yamauchi. Tokyo: Fukuinkan Shoten, 1999.

Summary:
In the mountain, there lived a poor old man alone. One winter evening, he heard a cat mewing at the door. The visitor was a wretched-looking black cat. This rude guest ate up all his scarce food. Meanwhile, the black cat, with the full stomach, began to groom himself. His fur, having been all wet and shabby, became puffed up and beautiful, and he purred. The old man burned all the firewood he had. He himself felt warm and comfortable and had a cozy time with the cat. He was so satisfied and peaceful that he forgot his hunger.

Next morning, when the cat went out, it turned to the old man and said, "Why didn't you drive me out?" The old man said, "No way! You and I haven't known each other, but now we are friends, aren't we?"

After he had parted from the cat, who went away without leaving any footprints on the snow, he went into the house and found abundant food and firewood and they were never eaten up or used up. The old man never saw the cat again, but, dozing near the fireplace, he sometimes heard the friend purring.

*   *   *

When I read this picture book, I was first impressed by the drawings of the cat. They are very realistic and depict the cat's true nature well. The pictures on the whole are painted in pale hues, and the black color of the cat is conspicuous. The outline of the shapes is vague, and so, in some pictures, the black cat looks as if it radiated a white aura, which seems to show the cat's mystique effectively.

This story can be read as "the cat's repayment of a favor to the kind old man." However, when I carefully thought about what the old man was really pleased with, another story came into shape.

It is true that the old man was given abundant food and firewood, but was it all he gained?

This story reaches a climax in the scene where the old man, answering the cat's question, says that he and the cat are *friends*. This scene suggests that this is a story of "friendship," rather than of "returning a favor."

Although this man is old and feels sorry for his poverty, he is not obsequious. He varies the pace of his life, such as setting a day in a week when he eats a delicious meal, and he lives a well ordered life with pride.

On the other hand, the black cat has a strong ego that can demand what it wants, green eyes which have insight into things and a dignity which arises from its elegant movement.

That is to say, true friendship is the relationships between the people who live with dignity and appreciate and respect each other like the old man and the cat.

The author chose a cat as the old man's friend from among many animals. I admit that no other animals claim equality with humans such as cats. Friendship is nurtured only in the equal relationships. This is the story of compensation of one friend to the other.

Thus, the author liberates the old man from the serious position of "a benefactor" in common stories of repayment, and changes him to be a lighter "friend." I was deeply moved that the old man became freer than before. It was a fresh excitement. It was as if I was liberated and relieved after unloading a heavy burden, or it was like a palpitation felt when you have found something nice unexpectedly.

However, this black cat was not his friend from the beginning. It transformed itself in his mind from a miserable stray cat to a companion with whom he shared a happy time, and at last to a respectful friend, proud like a queen.

When he parted from the cat, it was certainly his friend, so he was not surprised even if the cat spoke a human language. The friendship cherished between them will be an everlasting treasure in his heart.

I assume that what this old man has gained is not only a true friend but also the pleasure and pride that he has a friend.

This conviction will fill the old man's heart with warmth and give him strength to live on.

Works Consulted

Ainsworth, Ruth. "The Cat Visitor." *The Ten Tales of Shellover*. London: Deutsch, 1963. Harmondsworth: Puffin, 1979. 17-25.

---. *Kuroneko no Okyakusama* [The Cat Visitor] 黒ねこのおきゃくさま. Trans. Ara Konomi 荒このみ. Tokyo: Fukuinkan Shoten 福音館書店, 1999.

Chapter VI

Longing for Eternity   I
—What Has Arisen from the World of Lindgren's Works—

Astrid Lindgren
Bröderna Lejonhjärta   [The Brothers Lionheart]
Illustrated by Ilon Wikland
Stockholm: Rabén & Sjögren, 1973

* Japanese edition: Lindgren, Astrid. *Harukana Kuni no Kyodai*. Trans. Yuzo Otsuka. Tokyo: Iwanami Shoten, 1976.

On January 28, 2002, Astrid Lindgren departed this life at the age of ninety-four for the "land beyond the stars." She left an extensive collection of literature for children as she had continued to write for fifty-one years. The number exceeds eighty, and they were written in Swedish, her mother tongue, and were translated into some seventy languages. However, I had not had such a strong interest in Lindgren compared to other writers. Nevertheless, when I happened to read her *Bröderna Lejonhjärta* [The Brothers Lionheart] in Japanese translation, I felt both unusual excitement and a sort of surprise.

This novel is completely different from her most recognized works, *Pippi Långstrump* [Pippi Longstocking] series (1945–48). While I had felt I could not tolerate the heroine, Pippi's anarchic behaviors, I became interested in the author who wrote works with such remarkable amplitude.

I realized that I had little knowledge of Lindgren, when it chanced that her critical biography, *Pippi no Umino Oya: Asutoriddo Rindoguren* [Astrid Lindgren, the Creator of Pippi] written by Keiko Sampei, was published by Iwanami Shoten in 1999. According to Sampei, Lindgren's books are categorized into three groups. The first group consists of absurd adventures represented by *Pippi Longstocking*, the second, the stories set in her hometown in her youth, among which there are *Emil i Lönneberga* [Emil of Lönneberga] series and *Barnen i Bullerbyn* [Noisy Village] series, and the third, fantasies, including *The Brothers Lionheart* (165-66).

I classified the fantasies:

#1—The stories in which the protagonists go into the world of the dead out of the world of the living and come back.
Examples: *I Skymningslandet* [In the Land of Twilight], *Tu tu tu!* [The Sheep of Kapera[1]], *Junker Nils av Eka* [Junker Nils of Eka].

#2—The stories in which they go into the world of the dead and never come back.
Examples: *Mio, min Mio* [Mio, My Son], *Sunnanäng* [The Red Bird], *Spelar min lind, sjunger min näktergal* [My Nightingale is Singing], *The Brothers Lionheart*.

I am fascinated by the fantasies classified as #2, including *The Brothers Lionheart,* in which the protagonists travel into the world of the dead and never return.

Now, there are a variety of definitions of "fantasy." I consider it to be as follows:

"Children under an impasse have various experiences in the imaginary world apart from reality. These experiences make them grow and when they have come back to the real world, the impasse has been overcome." In other words, conventionally, fantasies are the stories in which living beings go to another world and come back. However, this definition cannot be applied to

The Brothers Lionheart by Lindgren. For, the brothers go into "Nangiyala," the other world, and never come back.

So, I would like to consider this story as "new fantasy," which brings in the world of the dead, going over the boundary of the traditional concept of fantasy. The works of this genre continued to be written persistently while the author was writing other works of different genre including *Mio, My Son*. I perceived intuitively that Lindgren, the creator of Pippi, pursued her own theme in the story of the death world in the category 2, and I wanted to find it.

First, I read Lindgren's works as a quick view. I observed the transition from *Pippi Longstocking* written at the age of thirty-seven to *Ronja Rövardotter* [The Robber's Daughter], at the age of seventy-four (Though the author of the critical biography categorized this work as a fantasy, I would rather consider it to be an adventure story, judging from the view point of whether it has "the world of the dead" or not).

When you look at Pippi and Ronja with "the world of the dead" in mind, Pippi is a girl who does not want to grow up, and Ronja is a young woman who has grown steadily from being a baby into a being who raises her voice of joy in the spring of life that comes about at last. After the three books in the Pippi series that were translated into Japanese, eight or so books were written (not translated into Japanese). The last one was written two years before *The Robber's Daughter* was written. This fact might suggest that Lindgren thought that the Pippi series had issues to be pursued as well as the stories of the world of the dead.

I will think of "growth" and "death."

Growth takes place naturally in the process of living toward death. "Not wanting to become an adult" could mean refusing to grow, which could be equal to not approaching death. Although I have no clear idea of whether the characteristics of Pippi described in earlier books and those in later books differ from each other or not, in *The Robber's Daughter* the author's attitude toward "death" and "growth" has greatly changed from that in the earlier works. I assume that the key which explains the change lies in *The Brothers Lionheart* written at the age of forty-four.

The Brothers Lionheart is a story about two brothers who save and are saved by each other in this world and the other world, Nangiyala, and both go on into the new world, Nangilima. By experiencing the adventures in Nangiyala they grow up spiritually as well as physically and gain eternal life as brave men.

That is to say, in this story Lindgren accomplished Pippi's wish for not becoming a grown-up and reached "an everlasting child." As long as we live in this world, growth is inevitable. However, children who died young never grow any more. The author, who has let her characters attain eternity made a complete change and accepted growth.

While *The Brothers Lionheart* can be considered an elder brother, *Mio, My Son* written when the author was forty-seven years old is a younger brother. According to the critical biography, two years before publication, her husband died from illness and her eldest son, Lars, got married and left her about this time (Sampei 47). This was the time for loss for the author. The boy protagonist of this story is nine years old and has been raised up by cruel foster parents. His mother has died at his birth. His father is not unknown. His foster parents hurt him by telling that his father must be a villain. One day, he goes on an errand and sets off for the other world, the world of the dead. The world is ruled by his father as a king, who loves him from the bottom of his heart. The boy now becomes Prince Mio and realizes his own mission, which is to retrieve the children who have been kidnaped by the evil knight with a stone heart and to give them back to their parents. Here, an issue between "the father and the child" is noticeably presented. In fact, Lindgren's son, Lars, had also been fostered out for some period. His father was not identified like the protagonist. According to the biographer, her son's father was probably the editor of a newspaper where she worked part-time after graduation (Sampei 29-30). Lindgren is said to have been raised by affectionate parents in a free atmosphere and to have had so happy a childhood that she *almost died from playing too much* (qtd. in Sampei 18). However, it is said that as she grew up, she stopped being "a good girl," and became a pleasure-seeking woman (Sampei 25). For Lindgren, growing up to be an adult whose freedom is restricted must have meant to move away from happiness.

Her father was a manager of a farm belonging to a church in the town (Sampei 14). It is natural that he should have had an inclination toward Christianity. In addition, it was in the 1920s, when an old order still dominated. It would have been difficult for her father to accept his daughter bearing an illegitimate child. There is a passage in *The Robber's Daughter*. One day, Ronja's mother visits her beloved daughter, who has run away from home and lives with her lover in the woods. Ronja has been disconnected with her father. She says, "Look, Lena [Ronja's mother], if you were a child and had a father who denied you so hard that he wouldn't even say your name, would you go back to him? Supposing he didn't even come and ask you?" (Crampton 157).

This reflects Astrid's true feelings as a daughter of her father, Samuel. She, as a daughter of a young generation, is not ashamed of her own conduct. In the end, Lindgren, who was eighteen years old, lost her father's protection, with a baby in her womb, and was obliged to start a single life. After giving birth, she had little income and found it hard to survive. In those circumstances, what was the consolation for a young woman who made a trip to and from Denmark to see her son? Books consoled her (Sampei 29-31). She ran into the library like a thirsty woman and tried to borrow some books like a drowning person needs something to cling to. There is an episode when she found it impossible to borrow books quickly due to rules, she burst into tears (qtd. in Sampei 31-32).

Lindgren had been good at writing since childhood (Sampei 23). It is proved by the fact that she wrote articles anonymously for the newspaper company where she worked part-time (Sampei 28). However, it was her father, who liked telling stories, who had built the foundation of her career as a writer. He told her folk tales and stories about the incidents in the district almost every night (Sampei 213). It is certain that Lindgren, who was full of curiosity, enjoyed these nights, judging from the fact that she herself loved collecting legends of the local community (Cott 223). In fact, she had a deep affection for her father. What threatened this strong bond between the father and the daughter was nothing but her growth. It was to lose freedom which she had enjoyed and to part from her father. It is said that in a TV interview she was unwilling to tell about those years, confessing that after the heavenly childhood her teen years had been boring to her (qtd. in Sampei 27).

Pippi believes that her father was hit by the storm during his voyage and is now the king of a country somewhere in the south and that he will come and fetch her (*Pippi Longstocking*). In her *Lillebror och Karlsson på taket* [Karlsson-on-the-Roof], Karlsson is a middle-aged dwarf, of her father's age. Karlsson tells Lillebror, a seven-year-old boy, to stay as a child forever. Children's growth is considered unfavorable. I think Pippi and Karlsson are the companions whom Lindgren created to heal her solitary urban life and to preserve the eternal child as a core in herself. Her deep yearning for her father is perceived in these stories of Pippi and Karlsson.

After a while, she got married and her life stabilized. She took back her son, and received numerous prizes (Sampei). It seems to mean that she had graduated from the state of eternal child. Although it is not clear when the reconciliation between the daughter and the father occurred, the last scene of *The Robber's Daughter* illustrates that it brought her a great delight after her long and distressful journey for independence. Ronja accepts her father's compromise and goes back to her father. She walks again in the woods with her lover in the spring which comes round soon:

> And they come to their cave, their home in the wilderness. And everything is as before, safe and familiar; the river rushing down below, the woods in the morning light, everything is the same as ever. The spring is new, but it is still the same as ever.
>
> 'Don't be scared, Burl [Birk],' says Kirsty [Ronja]. 'My spring yell is just coming!!'
>
> And she yells, shrill as a bird, a shout of joy which can be heard far away in the forest. (Crampton 191-92)

A fledgling, Pippi, has grown into a bird who sings out loud in the woods.

In *Pippi Longstocking*, *The Brothers Lionheart*, and then in *The Robber's*

Daughter, what Lindgren pursued consistently was the theme of "growth" and "death" and then "eternity." That emerged from the issue of "the father and the child" in her. In other words, they are the record of her long conflict in which she fought with her father and then won her independence from him. In that conflict, Lindgren, in order to keep mental balance, created stories the themes of which oscillate between adventures and the story of the death world.

Eternity means that life lasts forever, and I think all the human beings fear death from birth and wish to live forever.

The protagonists of the stories, indeed, are not conscious of the wish for eternity. It is felt by them as concrete wishes for "being a free child forever" or "living forever with people whom they love." However, at the bottom of their wishes there might be wishes for eternity that are possessed by us all.

In *Kodomo no Hon no 8nin* [Pipers at the Gates of Dawn] by Jonathan Cott, Lindgren says in the talk with the author of this book that she thought it was useless to be a writer and add one more book to a list of books already written. She refers to the Book of Ecclesiastes in the Old Testament (226). In fact, there is this passage in Chapter 12, Paragraph 12:

> Furthermore, my son, be admonished: of making many books there is no end; and much study is a weariness of the flesh. (*World English Bible*, Eccles. 12.12)

However, in Chapter 3, Paragraph 11 says:

> He has made everything beautiful in its time. He has also set eternity in their hearts. (Eccles. 3.11)

Yes. We cannot live forever, but we are given "eternity in our hearts." It was this wish for eternity that I believe motivated Lindgren to be the creator of stories.

Note

1. *Tu tu tu!*: The English title, "The Sheep of Kapera," is the translation from the title of the Japanese edition of *Tu tu tu!*

Works Consulted

Cott, Jonathan. *Kodomo no Hon no 8nin : Yoake no Fuefuki Tachi* 子どもの本の8人：夜明けの笛吹きたち. Trans. Suzuki Sho 鈴木晶. Tokyo: Shobunsha 晶文社, 1988. Trans. of *Pipers at the Gates of Dawn: The Wisdom of Children's Literature*. New York: Random, 1983.

Crampton, Patricia, trans. *The Robber's Daughter*. By Astrid Lindgren. London: Methuen Children's Books, 1983.

Lindgren, Astrid. *Bröderna Lejonhjärta* [The Brothers Lionheart]. Stockholm: Rabén & Sjögren, 1973.

---. *Harukana Kuni no Kyodai* [The Brothers Lionheart] はるかな国の兄弟. Trans. Otsuka Yuzo 大塚勇三. Tokyo: Iwanami Shoten 岩波書店, 1976.

---. *Karlsson på taket* [Karlsson-on-the-Roof]. Stockholm: Rabén & Sjögren, 1955.

---. *Mio, min Mio* [Mio, My Son]. Stockholm: Rabén & Sjögren, 1954.

---. *Pippi Långstrump* [Pippi Longstocking]. Stockholm: Rabén & Sjögren, 1945.

---. *Ronja Rövardotter* [The Robber's Daughter]. Stockholm: Rabén & Sjögren, 1981.

---. *Sanzoku no Musume Ronya* [The Robber's Daughter] 山賊のむすめローニャ. Trans. Otsuka Yuzo 大塚勇三. Tokyo: Iwanami Shoten 岩波書店, 2001.

Sampei, Keiko 三瓶恵子. *Pippi no Umino Oya*: *Asutoriddo Rindoguren* [Astrid Lindgren, the Creator of Pippi] ピッピの生みの親：アストリッド・リンドグレーン. Tokyo: Iwanami Shoten 岩波書店, 1999.

World English Bible. BibleGateway.com. 5 May 2016 <https://www.biblegateway.com>.

Chapter VII

Longing for Eternity II
—"The Eternal Child" in Lindgren—

Astrid Lindgren
Bröderna Lejonhjärta   [The Brothers Lionheart]
Illustrated by Ilon Wikland
Stockholm: Rabén & Sjögren, 1973

* Japanese edition: Lindgren, Astrid. *Harukana Kuni no Kyodai*. Trans. Yuzo Otsuka. Tokyo: Iwanami Shoten, 1976.

A longing for eternity may have been the driving force behind Lindgren's prolific output as an author. What made her long for eternity? What is the worth of eternity? Do we long for eternity because we, as mortal beings, want to live long? What is expressed by the word "eternity" might be a search for the everlasting values. In this chapter, I will explore the everlasting values which Lindgren sought for by investigating mainly *Bröderna Lejonhjärta* [The Brothers Lionheart], which seems to be the key to the transition from Pippi, who does not want to be an adult, to Ronja, who accepts growth.

I was moved most by the first chapter and the last chapter of *The Brothers Lionheart*. The story centers on two brothers: older Jonathan and younger, bed-ridden Rusky. In the first chapter, Jonathan, who is in grief over his own misfortune, says that when Rusky dies he will fly to the world called

Nangiyala, where he can take part in glorious adventures from morning till dusk. In comparison, he, Jonathan, will have to live without his beloved brother in this world like a jail. I was amazed by this argument because it went against everything I had considered a common belief until then. However, it has a strange power to persuade me. I marveled at the power of her expression that silenced me and left me in wonder.

In the last chapter, I was thrown into a panic, complete confusion. The two brothers are fatally injured in the last battle and help each other to throw themselves into the bottom of the unknown valley. It looks as if they committed double suicide. Can this be accepted as a book for children? I was never convinced of the last scene which could be interpreted as a glorification of death. Rusky utters a cry of joy in the dark on the way down to the bottom of the valley, "Oh, Nangilima! Yes, Jonathan. Yes. I can see the light! I can see the light!" (Tate 188). This last line of the book did not convince me.

The value that I expect from children's literature is "hope." Any unhappy ending can be accepted if it has some hope. I approve of children's literature with tough endings rather than easy, happy-endings. However, I could not accept the ending of this story. A big question for me is: Why did the author of Pippi write the story in which the protagonists felt happiness in death? This issue occupied my mind for a long time, which made me obsessed with this story.

After a while, when I finally gave up solving the question for myself, I reached an idea that I would ask about it directly to a Swede. Fortunately, there is Swedish Center Foundation[1] in Tobetsu town, near Sapporo. I was able to meet Helena Iida Björkman, a young Swedish project leader of the exchange activity. As a result, I found that the book has widespread, positive appeal in Sweden. She said that when it was published in 1973, it provoked arguments for and against. She, a young woman in her twenties, observed that this book was often read by mothers to their children to teach the reality of life and death and was often introduced in primary schools. She said that it was necessary even for little children to understand "death" and that this was an excellent book read for that purpose. She went on to say that in fact an acquaintance, whose elder brother had died from illness, had overcome his grief by reading *The Brothers Lionheart*.

In Sweden there are few steep mountains or valleys and, instead, there are woods, lakes or grass-covered plains. According to Ms. Björkman, the geographical features depicted as Nangiyala are considered to be exotic. While I looked over the materials about Scandinavia, I found that the description of Nangiyala is very similar to that of Iceland, a Scandinavian country like Sweden. Iceland is introduced in an electronic encyclopedia, *Maipedia* [My Pedia], as follows:

> It is an island in the northern Atlantic Ocean, located in the northwest of Europe. . . . It is surrounded by fjordic coasts and consists of plateaus six hundred meters high on average. There are many active volcanos such as Mt. Hecla, which produce plenty of hot springs. More than ten percent of the island is covered with glaciers. . . . Norwegians immigrated there around 874. . . . ("Aisurando")

I suppose that the model of Nangiyala with deep hollows, dizzying deep valleys, big mountains, rivers and waterfalls is Iceland. Adding to that, Iceland has an image of a mystic island. One writer called it a magical land. These images might be derived from its features which we find to be of another world and from its mysteriousness that we feel because it is the land where Norse mythology is living. Norse mythology is also called Germanic mythology, which ancient Germans believed. In the seventeenth century documents written in Old Icelandic were discovered and it produced a sensation. It is said that the mythologies were created more than thirty-two hundred years ago before the discovery (Shikaku Dezain Kenkyujo 106; Higashiura and Takemura, Foreword 5). In this respect, the mythology is both old and new.

The medieval period is the time when the Viking was dominant. Nangiyala, where the brothers make the adventure, is also in the age of knights. The Germanic people are the ancestors of Scandinavians, including Danes, Swedes, Norwegians and Icelanders, as well as the English, the German, and the Dutch. At that time, the chief god, Odin, was fervently worshiped by the Viking as a god of war. However, after they had ravaged Europe for one hundred and thirty years, they eventually encountered Christianity, and renounced their gods, one by one (Higashiura and Takemura, Commentary 280).

In the Norse mythology, there are stories of Balder, which strongly resemble *The Brothers Lionheart*. In the stories, the brothers die one after the other and reunite.

In Asgard, the world of the gods, live twins, Balder and Hoder. They are the sons of the supreme god, Odin. Balder is called the light of the summer and the most beautiful of the gods, and his beauty is compared to a white flower. He is very good at telling stories and is loved by everyone. He is the delight of the gods. (He resembles Jonathan in *The Brothers Lionheart*.) The younger brother, Hoder, is blind, and is of a pale presence. One day, he is used by Loki, an evil god, for hi trick, and accidentally kills his brother (Mackenzie, *Teutonic* 146-57). He can be compared to Rusky because he is going to die and feels lonely and helpless, so he wishes for his brother's death unconsciously, expecting his brother to go into Nangiyala first so that his brother can be waiting for him. This realization made me convinced that *The Brothers Lionheart* is modeled on Norse mythology. Both pairs of brothers meet again in the world of the dead, and in a while, they move on to another world: Balder and Hoder, from the underground up to the new plateau, and Jonathan and Rusky throw themselves down to Nangilima.

However, this interpretation posed further questions: why one ascends, and the other descends. Heaven has the image of "upwards" while "downwards" has only negative images such as hell, darkness and a prison. Therefore, it is not realistic to believe that the brothers will become happy. What does "downwards" actually mean to the brothers? In the last chapter, when Jonathan has been burnt by a monster, Katla's fire and has been nearly killed, he says, "I thought perhaps I could jump again. Down the precipice—down to a meadow" (Tate 186).

Here, we must recall that the brothers once jumped down. The fire at their apartment house took Jonathan's life. The reason Jonathan jumped down from the third floor of the house, with his younger brother on his back, was to escape from the fire and to survive together, not to die. As a consequence, they came to Nangiyala.

Nangiyala is considered to be in the distant past, and at the same time, in the recent past. It is in the past, far from the present time, when humans were healthier and freer, and they lived happily in the land full of nature. Judging from these descriptions, the brothers are going down to survive and the direction was toward the unknown and better world. There is a material which supports my assertion.

According to *Teutonic Myth and Legend*, written by Donald A. Mackenzie, in Norse mythology, people who have died go down to "Hela":

> Now in Hela is the lower-world Thingstead of the gods, where the souls of the dead are judged, and rewards and punishments are meted out by Odin. . . .
>
> Those who are justified pass to the eternal realms of Hela, where joy prevails. . . .
>
> The happy dead disport themselves on the green plains of Hela, where they meet lost friends and ancestors from the earliest years of the world. And many beauteous ways they travel, and wonderful tales they hear. The children are cared for in the realm of Mimer, "memory", where joy is theirs forever and their food is honey-dew. (15-18)

This description coincides with Nangilima that Jonathan describes. The image of Nangilima is also what Lindgren found in Norse mythology. The underground world is not pitch-dark, but a beautiful world, full of light and green.

"The Vala's Song" (*Völuspá*, the Seeress's Prophesy) in the documents of Norse mythology describes that the death of Balder is the omen for "Ragnarok," the destruction of the power of all things. After the death of Balder, the climate changes drastically, very severe winter strikes for three consecutive years. At the end of the desperate fights between gods and the giants and the monsters, they defeat each other and the world collapses. The old earth is burnt out and "sinks into Ocean," and "the giant wolf . . . swallows" the old Sun. However, the Sun's daughter, who was born just before the Sun's death, shines over the earth which have risen "from the deep sea." Then the brother gods, Balder and Hoder, who have come back from their dwelling in hell, resurrect (Mackenzie, *Teutonic* 146-57, 177-85). This means the loss and the restoration of light, that is, the replacement of the old world by the new world. People regard this evolution as the transition from the world of Norse mythology to that of Christianity (Higashiura and Takemura, Foreword 4-7). *Völuspá* itself is considered to be the record of the reorganization of the oral tradition by Christianized Icelanders (Higashiura and Takemura, Foreword 5; Mizuno 18-19, 21-22). With this in mind, the descent by Jonathan and Rusky might be interpreted as a step before an ascent. However, if Lindgren aims to make them continue descending, then, it might be "the eternal child" within her that wishes them to descend.

According to Lindgren, one evening, she, walking in a cemetery, found a little brothers' grave with the epitaph on it saying, "The little brothers rest here." Having seen it, she began to contemplate what had happened to them and why they had had to die young. These questions made her write this story. And after a while, when she saw a rosy sun rise in a winter morning, she was convinced of what she wanted to write (Cott 229-30). Scandinavian climate lacks light. The sun shines for only several months, or, depending on the conditions, for only several weeks. For the people who live in this severe environment, spring, when light returns after the long winter, is the time when the lives of all living things revive. She intuited that the children who were destined to die soon needed hope and salvation more than anything else. This belief made her look back to her happy past and onward to the stories of the past when Norse mythology was believed.

Now, if Nangilima can be identified as "Hela," the paradise, then why is it necessary for the brothers of *BL* to travel in Nangiyala before Nangilima? The brothers are not evil, but, I would suggest, the younger, Rusky, is very cowardly. However, his cowardliness serves a narrative purpose.

According to Mackenzie, in order to avoid going to "Nifel-hel," where torments and punishment wait, people must "have been honourable and full of pity and have helped others; because they were brave and feared not to die" (*Teutonic* 17). Compared to his elder brother, Rusky would not have satisfied these conditions. It might have been necessary for him, who was not courageous enough, to go to Nangiyala, experience the adventures and become a brave knight who can save his brother and other people.

What Rusky needs is courage. After the numerous challenges, the younger makes his older sibling call him "Brave little Rusky." His strong wish to rescue his brother urges him to be courageous and take action. What makes people take action is not power.

The original title of this book is *Bröderna Lejonhjärta* [The Brothers Lionheart]. Lionheart means courage. The courage with which the elder boy sacrifices his own life to save his brother and the younger jumps down to Nangilima might be the source of this title.

This self-sacrifice is a value common to Christianity and Norse mythology: Odin in Norse mythology is the god of war and demands human life as a proof of loyalty to him, and in Christianity, Jesus was crucified on the cross to redeem human sin.

It may be possible to assume that Lindgren, fighting against her father's values (Christianity) through the creation of children's literature, found the commonality between Christianity and Norse mythology, and that it paved the way to the reconciliation with her father.

This story takes place in the world of the dead, which we cannot perceive. She succeeded in unfolding the amazingly concrete image of another world, making the most use of her abundant imagination lined with Norse mythology. The days of thrilling adventures depicted in this story engender hope and courage in the mind of a dying child, to jump into the unknown world without fear. It might be for this purpose that this story was written.

To solve the mystery of this story, I looked at her works and found that her works deeply connect to her life. Parting from her father, giving birth to her illegitimate child, fostering her child out, getting married, a debut as a writer, taking back her son, the reconciliation with her father and her husband's death—these incidents cast their shadows on her works. With her life experiences in mind, I wondered why Lindgren longed for eternity, and I concluded that it was to keep her balance in both body and mind. It is said that she was emotionally changeable (Sampei 215). We can observe it in her works: absurdity, anarchism, humor and mischief abound in her thrilling stories.

What did she desire with such ardent temperament within her? I think she wanted to return to her childhood. In *Kodomo no Hon no 8nin* [Pipers at the Gates of Dawn] by Jonathan Cott, Lindgren says, yearning for her childhood, that her parents were beside her whenever she wanted them to and that they otherwise let her loiter around fascinating playgrounds (222). She goes on to say that she can recall what she sensed in her childhood as if it were happening then, and she reflects that it was a long time ago and wonders where all have gone (231-32).

Our life is succession of ups and downs. Big waves and small waves continuously assail us. Sometimes we manage to let the wave pass, and sometimes we lose our balance. In such occasion, we try to invent our own way to keep balance.

In Chapter VI, I wrote that her works were the record of her conflict to win her independence from her father. Like Pippi, Lindgren refused to grow and did not want to give away "the eternal child" inside her, but she could provide Jonathan and Rusky, whose growth is prevented by death, with their last peaceful dwelling. Their joy bears fruit in the later story of Ronja, a daughter who becomes independent from her father.

The worth of eternity that Lindgren longed for was "the absolute peacefulness at heart," which she had been given in her childhood. The sense of happiness which she had lost as she grew was symbolized as "the eternal child" within her, and she continued to pursue it in her writing of children's literature.

Notes

1. Swedish Center Foundation
   2-3-1 Sweden Hills Village, Tobetsu-cho, Ishikari-gun, Hokkaido

Works Consulted

"Aisurando" [Iceland] アイスランド. *Maipedia* [My Pedia] マイペディア. Tokyo: Heibonsha 平凡社, 1994.

Cott, Jonathan. *Kodomo no Hon no 8nin : Yoake no Fuefuki Tachi* 子どもの本の8人：夜明けの笛吹きたち. Trans. Suzuki Sho 鈴木晶. Tokyo: Shobunsha 晶文社, 1988. Trans. of *Pipers at the Gates of Dawn: The Wisdom of Children's Literature.* New York: Random, 1983.

Higashiura, Yoshio 東浦義雄, and Takemura Etsuko 竹村恵都子. Commentary. Mackenzie, *Hokuo no Roman* 275-316.

---. Foreword. Mackenzie, *Hokuo no Roman* 1-10.

Lindgren, Astrid. *Bröderna Lejonhjärta* [The Brothers Lionheart]. Stockholm: Rabén & Sjögren, 1973.

---. *Harukana Kuni no Kyodai* [The Brothers Lionheart] はるかな国の兄弟. Trans. Otsuka Yuzo 大塚勇三. Tokyo: Iwanami Shoten 岩波書店, 1976.

Mackenzie, Donald A. *Hokuo no Roman: Geruman Shinwa* [Teutonic Myth and Legend] 北欧のロマン：ゲルマン神話. Trans. Higashiura Yoshio 東浦義雄, and Takemura Etsuko 竹村恵都子. Tokyo: Taishukan Shoten 大修館書店, 1997.

---. *Teutonic Myth and Legend.* London: Gresham, 1912. *sacred-texts.com.* 15 May 2016 <http://sacred-texts.com/neu/tml/index.htm>.

Mizuno, Tomoaki 水野知昭. *Sei to Shi no Hokuo Shinwa* [Life and Death in Norse Mythology] 生と死の北欧神話. Tokyo: Shohakusha 松柏社, 2002.

Sampei, Keiko 三瓶恵子. *Pippi no Umino Oya: Asutoriddo Rindoguren* [Astrid Lindgren, the Creator of Pippi] ピッピの生みの親：アストリッド・リンドグレーン. Tokyo: Iwanami Shoten 岩波書店, 1999.

Shikaku Dezain Kenkyujo 視覚デザイン研究所, ed. *Vinasu no Kataomoi: Shinwa no Mei Shinshu* [Venus's Unrequited Love: The Collection of Impressive

Scenes in Myths] ヴィーナスの片思い：神話の名シーン集. Tokyo: Shikaku Dezain Kenkyujo 視覚デザイン研究所, 1995.

Tate, Joan, trans. *The Brothers Lionheart*. By Astrid Lindgren. Oxford UP, 2009.

Chapter VIII

Building Up an Image of an Independent Woman
—What Does *The Yearling* Mean to Rawlings?—

Marjorie Kinnan Rawlings
The Yearling
New York: Scribner's, 1938

* Japanese edition: Rawlings, Marjorie Kinnan. *Kojika Monogatari*. Trans. Hisashi Shigeo. Tokyo: Obunsha, 1968.

The Yearling, which depicts a boy's affection for a fawn, is widely accepted as a classic of American children's literature. While most of the editions we read in Japan are digests from the original, the complete translation has about 600 pages in a pocket edition, and the content of the story is more complicated than that given in the digests.

The author, Marjorie Kinnan Rawlings, wrote this book not only for children, but also she intended to make it worth reading to adults. This book won the Pulitzer Prize[1] for the Novel in 1939. I first read a version with 320 pages published by Popurasha, and later I was able to read a version published by Obunsha with twice as many pages as the previous one.

I was puzzled by the protagonist's mother, Ora. Her pessimistic views, coldheartedness and lack of sympathy as well as her persistence in eating amazed me. I will quote her words which illustrate her personality:

The conversation with her son, Jody:
Ora: "I should jest say not. What you mean, milk a-plenty? They ain't a extry drop left from sun to sun."
Jody: "It could have my milk."
Ora: "Yes, and fatten the blasted fawn and you grow up puny."
Jody: "I want one. . . . I jest want something. . . . I jest want something all my own. Something to foller me and be mine." "I want something with dependence to it."
Ora: "Well, you'll not find that no-where. Not in the animal world nor in the world o' man" (Rawlings, *The Yearling* 117).

When she is told by her husband, Penny, about the death of Fodder-wing, who is Jody's only friend:
Ora: "Well—Pity 'twa'n't that great quarrelin' Lem."
Penny: "I never seed a family take a thing so hard."
Ora: "Don't tell me them big rough somebodies took on" (240).

To Jody:
"You and them hounds and all the rest o' the stocks mighty lovin' on a empty belly and me with a dish in my hand" (38).

To Jody and Penny:
"Meat now, and none this winter."
"Nobody but me don't take life serious" (42).

This story deals with the time about 70 years before Rawlings wrote it, and the setting is in the backwoods of Florida. The old way of life still survived there even when the author moved there in 1928.

Rawlings and America
Among her contemporaries was the American-born, British poet, T. S. Eliot.

He published a long poem, *Waste Land*, in 1922. He received the Nobel Prize and the poem is called a monumental work of modern literature. It had a great impact and influence on his contemporaries ("Eriotto").

According to *Maipedia* [My Pedia], Eliot, in this poem, "compared the circumstances of Europe after World War I to a wasteland and made its desolation stand out macroscopically, using ancient and medieval fertility mythologies as a framework and quoting from literary works and other literary sources of all times, and, at the same time, intimated his attitude about searching for salvation" ("Arechi").

American history is a history of a persevering cultivation of wilderness. They say that if civilization advances too far, human spirits will decay, which leads them to desire to return to nature and sound spirit of the past. I can perceive this desire in *The Yearling*, in the attitudes of Penny and the author, Rawlings, who turned their back to civilization and headed for the wasteland.

It is said that Rawlings aspired to be a novelist when her early novel was awarded a prize in a competition in her girlhood (Nagaoka and Tsuboi 133), but it was difficult for female writers to support themselves by writing novels in those days.

Rawlings was one of the writers in the 1930s, which is considered to be the golden age of American literary history. Her works were all published by Charles Scribner's Sons. The person in charge of her was M. E. Perkins, who is considered to be a legendary editor. He is famous for introducing Fitzgerald, Hemingway, Thomas Wolf and others to the world. It was after quitting the activities as a journalist in New York at the age thirty-two and moving to Cross Creek, Florida that Rawlings achieved success as a writer. The reason for her moving to Florida was to create good literary works more than else, and she found it to be a good environment ("Nenpu" 336). It is said that she had to fight against predicament for five years before she came into luck. Her pride, however, in living as an independent woman made her stay at Cross Creek (Rawlings, *Cross Creek*).

Women and Water

What Rawlings did first when she moved to Florida was to get a good supply of water just as all human have first sought for water to survive, illustrated in the fact that civilization emerged near big rivers (*Cross Creek*).

One of the reasons Ora in *The Yearling* is excessively coldhearted might be that she lives in the place not appropriate for living. What Ora vents one day hurts Penny's heart:

Ora says, "I'd not know what 'twas, not to be sparin' o'my water. For twenty years, I been sparin'" (95).

Penny is shocked by Ora's words and says to his son:

> " . . . . Ever' spring, I'd figger to git your Ma a well dug. Then I'd need a ox, or the cow'd bog down and perish, or one of the young uns'd put in and die and I'd have no heart for well-diggin'. . . . But twenty years is too long to ask ary woman to do her washin' on a seepage hillside." (101)

Penny's repentance might come from his decision made without thinking much of his wife's opinion. He decided that the plateau called Pine Island, which was a little higher in the thicket, would be the only suitable place for their life. The plateau where pines grew was drier than other wet lands and had a good view. Instead of choosing areas with a creek or a well, Penny chose to live with his family at a place drier even though it was inconvenient for them to get water and unfertile, and he later regrets it. I find self-centeredness in his decision. He gave priority to his preference and values.

This seems to have been brought by his selfishness; neglecting his family's inconvenience, he forces them to accept his preference. It was in the 1890s, when women's independence was not respected and Ora could not help but obey her husband.

Her sacrifice, however, was much greater than her husband had expected.

Ora's Sacrifice

It is the deaths of their five children that deprives her of warmth, a young and healthy woman who has been asked by her husband to move from a town to the frontier. Ora is a big woman, twice as big as little Penny, and bears babies, but they get ill and die soon. To protect their graves which are added year after year from the wild animals, they build a fence around them. Jody is the only child, but actually the sixth child. Ora's harshness toward her only son might be explained by her misfortune she has suffered for seven years.

Although the author says that Ora is a fictional character (S. Yoshida 332), I have come to believe that she is a compound of some real women after referring to some materials.

Models for Penny and Ora 1

"Antses in Tim's Breakfast" in *Cross Creek*, her autobiographical account of her relationships with her neighbors, depicts an incident that really happened. The woman in the episode who obeys her young husband, Tim, is one of the women Rawlings met at Cross Creek. Tim is a poor-white worker (cracker), and is so proud that he selects what jobs he will do and never does what hurts his pride. His wife is obliged to live an unstable life, even without drinking water near their residence. Her children do not grow well and soon die. Rawlings attempts to help her by asking her to help with her housework, but Tim gets infuriated that a white woman employs his wife as a maid, as she is also a white (in fact, partly native-American). Tim himself quit the job as a day-laborer at Rawlings's orange farm and disappears with his wife.

The husband and wife left a strong impression on Rawlings. And they were followed as a pattern. The diverse variations appear in her short stories. They are the stories of unstable lives brought about by a proud men and the existence of their obedient wives.

Models of Penny and Ora 2

Another example of this pattern is the old couple, Mr. and Mrs. Battler, whom Rawlings asked to raise her pigs at their farm. When she went to Mr. Battler's farm, he somehow invites her to pick beans under the moon light, and he says his bliss is to harvest the crop on his farm with his friends. The old wife cannot bear the lonely life and dreams of selling the land to someone and leaving, but the husband clings to his land and adamantly insists on defending the independent life (Rawlings, *Cross Creek* Chap. 19). The difference in their sense of values is clearly presented here. The husband attaches values on his own satisfaction rather than on his wife's happiness.

Models of Penny and Ora 3

The last example of this pattern is the relationships between Perkins, the editor in charge of Rawlings, whom I have mentioned before, and his wife. Although the two were from the same area and fell in love with each other in their high school days, they had completely different sense of values and they did not change nor compromise. It seems that the gap between them continued to widen until they died. It is rumored that Perkins was misogynist, but he was an attractive and talented editor. It is said that many writers adored him as if he was their second father and relied on him. He is said to have been a typical man from the North, a gentleman who was sincere, modest, sympathetic and quiet; whereas his wife Louis, becomes frustrated after her desire to become a stage actress is blocked by her husband and it caused frictions between the two. She became eccentric, being involved deeply in religion or addicted to alcohol (Nagaoka and Tsuboi 177-213; Berg 1: 54-56, 59-63, 162, 170-71, 205-14, 306, 353-57, 361-63; Berg 2: 14-28, 42, 83, 97-100, 129, 177-79, 276, 340-41). This might be seen as a state of a wife who has given in to her husband's strong will and lost her balance physically and mentally without being able to give up her dream.

Perkins and *The Yearling*

A gifted writer, Thomas Wolf, whom Perkins was in charge of, agreed to his advice to revise his massive work and reduce his usual volume. When his work was finally published, Wolf could not persuade himself that his work had been rightly trimmed by Perkins. Wolf sent a letter to break off his relationship with Perkins. Although the degree was slighter, it might be said that Rawlings was obliged to alter the plan of her work following Perkins's values. According to one account, she earlier wrote enthusiastically what is called Gothic novels, horror or mysterious stories set in medieval castles and etc. Perkins, however, did not approve the works that she sent him many times. In the meantime, he was impressed by the descriptions of rural life in Florida that Rawlings wrote about in her letters. He persistently persuaded her to write a story of a boy who lived there. Rawlings was not persuaded at first, for she was writing a novel, *Golden Apples*, about an Englishman. This novel, however, was received unfavorably and did not sell well. Rawlings, knowing that what she had wanted to write was not accepted by the readers, became disappointed and decided to take Perkins's advice. Thus, *The Yearling* was born.

Rawlings and Perkins took two years for planning and she wrote it, shutting herself up for one year. She bet her life as a writer on this work, but she became pessimistic about everything on the way and disposed of all of what she had written. She confessed in her letters that her agony in writing this story tempted her to alcohol, or induced her to reach a gun (Nagaoka and Tsuboi 111-30, 133-53; Berg 2: 107-11, 122-23). I presume that the cause was that she was forced to write what contradicted her sense of values. If it is true, she herself could be said to have been yet another model of Ora.

A Man's Pride and a Woman's Richness

From what I have written, I recognize that the women are deprived of their originally gifted physical and mental richness under the circumstances where men's pride or their sense of values have priority over women's, and they are compelled to live in environments without sufficient water to live. The seriousness of it is presented in the epilogue of *The Yearling* where Penny asks Jody, who has matured after experiencing hunger and betrayal in life:

> " . . . . I'd be proud to see the day when you got a well dug, so's no woman here'd be obliged to do her washin' on a seepage hillside. You willin'?" (470)

Here, the man admits his mistake he has made about women and asks the next generation to correct it.

The Author's Comments

Rawlings writes comments on *The Yearling* in the 1941 edition that Baxter Ma, who curses and swears, is a fictional character created from all nagging wives and mothers, and that as her writing proceeded, she realized how harsh life was to such women and what wounds in their hearts were hidden in their curses. Rawlings also expresses her sympathy for such a woman and confesses that she could not treat her as severely as planned at the beginning (qtd. in S. Yoshida 332).

Thus, it seems that Ora unexpectedly shook and altered the author's views about women. Although she began writing *The Yearling* strongly urged by Perkins, it grew to be a story for herself (Nagaoka and Tsuboi 135). That might be because Ora is a character whom Rawlings herself has created by weaving the female models mentioned before.

The Women in *The Yearling*

I was, at first, puzzled that all the women in *The Yearling* were unfavorable to some extent. However, it might be a matter of course because the women—Ora, a somewhat selfish relative, Hutto, who is one of her relatives, Twink, who is her son's capricious love, Eulalie, the daughter of a grocer in the town, who is compared to a snake, and the rude wives of the Forresters—all do not reach the high standard of independence that Rawlings attained. The only woman that is depicted as favorable is Nellie Ginright, who was once Penny's love but got married to other man and now is a widow. She is cheerful and lives in a house overlooking the river. She is divorced, lives alone in a house and supports herself. These circumstances are very similar to Rawlings's.

While Rawlings felt sympathy with people of the same sex who were obliged to obey their husbands, she never approved it. That might be because Ora, for Rawlings, was not strong or independent enough to get away from or improve the unsatisfactory environment.

I feel frustrated that Ora did not resist his husband when their second or third child died, before she lost five children. If she had imagined her own state in the future when she would have lost her richness, she would have bravely left the inhospitable pine island, instead of enduring so long. Although Ora expressed her complaint in her ironic remarks or talking to herself, she was not able to express herself logically. Even so, she could have shouted, "I cannot live at a place like this!"

Penny sought for peacefulness in his heart in a deserted place, being hurt by the conflicts between the people in the town, or their dishonesty and rudeness. His sensitivity would have perceived her plea if only she had raise her voice.

What Ora needed might be to present her will without suppressing it inside her and to propose an environment she wished for. If she still had to live in a remote place, she should have created her own pleasure. I am sorry that Ora did not have ideas or means to light her life, such as putting wild flowers on the table or keeping small animals as pets.

Junko Yoshida, who teaches British literature at Kobe Jogakuin University, writing in her *Amerika Jido Bungaku: Kazoku Sagashi no Tabi* [American Children's Literature: Quest for a family], unfolds her criticism on children's literature from the perspective of American history. She says that wives in the pioneering days can be classified as "pioneer wives," and that Laura's mother, Caroline, in *The Little House* books (1932–43), is representative of this. However, in *These Happy Golden Years* (1943), one of *The Little House* books, there is a character, Mrs. Brewster, with a contrasting personality to Caroline. She has also come to the frontier following her husband, and is an unhappy woman who cannot be independent in the severe life in the frontier and falls into insanity. Yoshida names Mrs. Brewster and Ora in *The Yearling* "angry pioneer women," and says that Ora's constant irritation is, in fact, to herself [who is indecisive and inactive]. This indication was highly satisfactory to me.

Ora and Jody

I contend that the death of Ora's five children lies at the back of her cold-heartedness. While I can understand her unconscious anger which lies in her against Penny, who put her in the barren environment, I could not understand well her indifference toward her innocent son. In spite of that, I now think as follows:

Jody was born. Ora thought that this baby would die soon, so that she did not expect much from nor love him. But he did not die and grew to be two years old. While she was confused and undecided whether she should unfasten the armor of her mind or not, the war started. Her husband said it would soon end, but the mother and the son lived at their acquaintance's in town, with the Hattos', during the four years of the Civil War. Ora did not enjoy life with the feminine old lady who was quite contrary to Ora. And the days in fear for her husband's death in the war did not make her loosen the armor in her mind. The war ended. Her husband took back his wife and his son to the pine island. Penny doted on Jody, now seven years old, being both a father and a mother to his son. While Ora remained armored in her mind, the son became his father's only child. The only reason for her existence now is in providing them with food. She became a nagging woman who boasts of her cooking, expecting gratitude in return from her husband and her son. She does not allow her son to keep a pet, and grudges food to it. Because of his mother's cold-heartedness, he fills the emptiness, which he could not share with his father, with the fawn. However, after one year, the fawn has grown and begins to damage their farm products. He shoots the fawn. That was a sad parting for the boy, who has grown up, from the fawn.

One Step Toward Independence

Penny says:

> " . . . . 'Tis fine, boy, powerful fine, but 'tain't easy. Life knocks a man down. . . ."
>
> [. . .]

". . . . But ever' man's lonesome. . . . Why, take it for his share and go on." (Rawlings, *The Yearling* 469-70)

Here I was dissatisfied with the author because Rawlings was on the side of Penny, not of Ora. I have felt in my everyday life the same sentiment as Ora feels, namely being unable to resist another person's values. However, reminding me of the fact that family members live together where their values confront each other, I feel I might also be a self-righteous Penny without knowing it.

Rawlings might have been a Penny in her behavior and an Ora in her sentiment. With this in mind, Penny's compassionate words to Ora and Ora's bitter words could be understandable. Humans wish to live with self-respect at times, and what supports it is a comfortable environment. Rawlings endeavored to attain a proper balance between her pride and surviving, but she didn't seem to have succeeded in it yet. That might be proved in the fact that she, after writing several works, proceeded on to writing Ellen Glasgow's biography.

Ellen Glasgow is an American female writer, twenty-three years older than Rawlings. She wrote *Barren Ground*, which is thought to be her most important work. It is a story about Dorinda, who studies scientific knowledge of agriculture in the city, and changes the barren land in her hometown into a productive land by soil improvement. We can see the firm determination, the execution and the reform by a woman who struggled to get away from the barren environment. And she took in her unfaithful ex-lover from a poorhouse and attended his deathbed. We can also see human love she managed to reach after overcoming her hatred against the person who had betrayed her. That is just what Ora could not do and what Rawlings wanted Ora to achieve. Judging from the course of her writing, I believe that Rawlings continued to create her works, aiming at more perfect independence, and *The Yearling* was the first step of it.

Notes

1. The Pulitzer Prizes: "an award for an achievement in American journalism, literature, or music. There are thirteen made each year" ("The Pulitzer Prizes").

Works Consulted

"Arechi" [Waste Land] 荒地. *Maipedia*.

Berg, Andrew Scott. *Mei Henshusha Pakinzu: Sakka no Saino o Hikidasu* 名編集者パーキンズ：作家の才能を引きだす. Trans. Suzuki Chikara 鈴木主税. 2 vols. Tokyo: Soshisha 草思社, 1987. Trans. of *Max Perkins: Editor of Genius*. New York: E. P. Dutton, 1978.

Cooke, Alistair. *Amerika: Kono Kyodaisa no Monogatari* アメリカ：この巨大さの物語. Trans. Suzuki Kenji 鈴木健次 and Sakurai Motoo 桜井元雄. Tokyo: Nihon Hoso Shuppan Kyokai 日本放送出版協会, 1978. Trans. of *Alistair Cooke's America*. London: British Broadcasting Corporation, 1973.

Cross Creek. Dir. Martin Ritt. Universal, 1983.

"Eriotto" [Thomas Stearns Eliot] エリオット. *Maipedia*.

Glasgow, Ellen Anderson Gholson. *Barren Ground*. New York: Doubleday, 1925.

---. *Fumo no Daichi* [Barren Ground] 不毛の大地. Trans. Itabashi Yoshie 板橋好枝. Tokyo: Arechi Shuppansha 荒地出版社, 1995.

Goldsmith, Oliver. *Dobutsushi* 動物誌. Trans. Tamai Tosuke 玉井東助. Tokyo: Hara Shobo 原書房, 1994. Trans. of *A History of the Earth and Animated Nature*. London: J. Nourse 1774.

Maipedia [My Pedia] マイペディア. Tokyo: Heibonsha 平凡社, 1994.

Nagaoka, Sadao 永岡定夫, and Tsuboi Kiyohiko 坪井清彦. *Tensai no Hakken: Mei Henshusha Makkusuweru Pakinzu to Sono Sakkatachi* [The Discovery of Genius: An Able Editor, Maxwell Perkins, and His Writers] 天才の発見：名編集者マックスウェル・パーキンズとその作家たち. Tokyo: Arechi Shuppansha 荒地出版社, 1983.

"Nenpu" [Chronological Record of Rawlings] 年譜. Chronological Record. Vol. 2 of *Kojika Monogatari*. By Rawlings. 336-38.

"The Pulitzer Prizes." *The Oxford Dictionary of English.* 2nd revised ed. 2005.

Rawlings, Marjorie Kinnan. *Cross Creek*. New York: Scribner's, 1942.

---. *Kojika Monogatari* [The Yearling] 子鹿物語. Trans. Shigeo Hisashi 繁尾久. 2 vols. Tokyo: Obunsha 旺文社, 1968.

---. *Suigo Monogatari* [Cross Creek] 水郷物語. Trans. Murakami Hiroo 村上啓夫. Tokyo: Hayakawa Shobo 早川書房, 1951.

---. *The Yearling*. 1938. New York: Scribner Paperback Edition, 2002.

Wilder, Laura Ingalls. *Kono Tanoshiki Hibi* この楽しき日々. Trans. Taniguchi Yumiko 谷口由美子. Tokyo: Iwanami Shoten 岩波書店, 2000. Trans. of *These Happy Golden Years.* New York: Harper and Brothers, 1943.

---. *The Little House* books. 8 vols. New York: Harper and Brothers, 1932-43.

Yoshida, Junko 吉田純子. *Amerika Jido Bungaku: Kazoku Sagashi no Tabi* [American Children's Literature: Quest for a family] アメリカ児童文学：家族探しの旅. Kyoto: Aunsha 阿吽社, 1992.

Yoshida, Shin'ichi 吉田新一. "Sakusha to Sakuhin ni tsuite" [About the Author and Her Works] 作者と作品について. Commentary. *Kojika Monogatari* [The Yearling] 子鹿物語. By Marjorie Kinnan Rawlings. Trans. Sugiki Takashi 杉木喬. Tokyo: Popurasha ポプラ社, 1969. 327-34.

Chapter IX

The Ability of Severance and the Future
—*Ai's Left Side*—

"With him always walking on my left side, I realized that he tried to protect me because my left hand didn't work well."

—Yasutaka Tsutsui, *Ai no Hidarigawa*

Yasutaka Tsutsui
Ai no Hidarigawa [Ai's Left Side]
Illustrated by Takahiro Asano
Tokyo: Iwanami Shoten, 2002

I. Expecting a New Image of Femininity

I have long had a tendency to distrust men. I do not distrust so much a boy or an old man as the men of ages between them. The cause is obvious. It is because I could not respect my father. As I did not like my father, who was the nearest man to me, I came to regard men in general as absurd, selfish, lacking in compassion and irresponsible.

With a longing for an ideal father in mind, I became sensitive to the fathers in children's literature.

Ai no Hidarigawa [Ai's Left Side] by Yasutaka Tsutsui attracted my interest because it is a story of a girl looking for her father. The protagonist, Ai, however, cannot find an ideal father. On the contrary, at the end of the story, she severs relations with her father one-sidedly after they had reunited at long last. It seems that the girl's growth is expressed in the acquisition of her ability to sever relations with her father. More surprisingly, she intentionally sows a seed of a conflict between two key male characters.

I could not fully endorse this scene, but, at the same time, I felt so exhilarated: I was astonished by this scene and doubted if the heroine of a book for children is permitted to do such a malicious act, however I also felt that was what I would have wanted to do and was greatly satisfied.

Ai's Character

Before Ai sets off on a journey of looking for her father, she does well at school and is pretty, and, because of that, she is bullied by her classmates, but she is tough and speaks back to her tormenters and to her inner self.

Moreover, when Ai's mother talks about her father who disappeared three years ago, "Your dad was weak, and he was an embarrassment to his family and to himself to have been deceived and have had his store taken, so he might be working somewhere to get back on his feet," she feels resentment against him and wants to scold him for abandoning her and the family. When she decides to run away from home, she says to herself, "If I cannot find my father, I will look for my happiness on my own." She doesn't depend on her father.

Looking for Her Father

What urges Ai to set off on a journey to look for her father is her mother's sudden death. She is badly treated and cheated by her mother's employer, who steals money left for her education. Unable to endure the predicaments, she sets off for Tokyo, leaving Hagi-cho, her hometown.

The Power of Animals

Ai is protected by Dane, a female Great Dane. Ai's mother asked the dog to protect her daughter and Ai has an ability to communicate with her protector. However, after three years, just after Ai has met her father, her ability to discern dogs' language disappears. It might suggest that Ai has grown up to be a woman who no longer needs maternal protection.

The Near-Future and an Old Man

This story is set in the time when one hundred-thousand-yen bills and electric cars are widely used. The author is writing this novel in the style of science fiction in which he imagines what will happen if only the negative parts of our current reality are allowed to develop: the contamination of the earth continues to get worse and the people's warm-heartedness is lost, and self-centeredness prevails. Security deteriorates: killing, robbing, and quarrels between ethnic groups occur night and day. People organize vigilante groups, and rich people guard themselves by hiring police officers as their body guards.

While Ai is running away from the vigilantes sent by her former employer, she is separated from Dane, and she is just luckily saved by an old man. This retired person admires Ai, who is travelling alone looking for her father, and becomes a companion of her journey and a guard.

The most significant role that he plays for her is that of an educator. He gives Ai the knowledge about some patterns of negative men in this world and how to deal with these men, besides educating her about languages, calculation, history and etc. (I mean by "negative men" the men with wickedness against women.)

Examples of Negative Men

#1—An overprotective father: Roku-san, whose daughter, Utako, is the meaning of his life and tries to lock her up in his house for ever.

#2—A man with Lolita complex: Gan, who tries to attack Ai, as an object of his sexual desire.

#3—Men who contaminate the earth: the men at Matsumura Kogyo Company, who cast away industrial waste for moneymaking.

#4—Youngsters who drive recklessly: Yamato and Jun, small-time yakuza, and Shirogumi and Makotogumi, motorcycle gangs.

#5—Men who do not carry out their duty of protectors: Ai's father, who does not communicate with Ai, and Hidetomo, the shop-keeper who does not allow Ai to go to school.

#6—A man who tries to dispel his own complex by attacking the weaker: Mr. Kinosita, who uses violence or violent words on Shizue.

In the story, the overprotective father in #1 has his daughter kidnapped by the motorcycle gangs and he is shot with a gun and dies. The man with Lolita complex in #2 is killed by the retired man who tries to protect Ai. The reason for #1 and #2 may be that those men are considered to be evil and that they should be obliterated. As for #3, it is the community that employs the dishonest trader, rather than an individual. The reaction in #4 is surprising. The retired man does not consider the small-time gang to be very evil and says, "They are naive enough to be deceived." This shows that the retired man was once one of them and knows well about the evil. That is why he can estimate the degree of evil.

Based on this consideration, you can see that the old man's indulgence toward the gang, Makotogumi, who kills the overprotective father and kidnaps Utako, and his rigidness toward the father are the two sides of the same idea. The author expresses his own view of fathers, using the image of the retired old man. According to his view, a father who does not lead his children toward independence should be rejected. This view is supported by his belief that a father's role is to give his children education and make them independent.

This idea helps understand the patterns #5 and #6. Those two are in cahoots. Although they are guardians or quasi-guardians, they are negative men who abandon their responsibility for giving their children the chance for education or depriving the environment of education of them.

In #6, Mr. Kinoshita, who lives with Shizue, is nagging and querulous because of his unsuccessful work and from his inferiority complex regarding his wife's better education level. He is a negative man who tries to hold onto a superior position by using a vulgar words or violence.

Parody

Generally speaking, the characters in this story have no depth. They exist there only to play their parts. Ai's role is to play a part of a girl who has lost her guardian. Satoru's role is to play a part of a boy who encourages the girl. The negative men are simply bad guys. They are negative elements of men. Utako and Shizue play the parts of their victims. Thus, *Ai's Left Side*, where characters play the exaggerated and distorted parts, is a parody that satirizes a contemporary society in which the male-dominated regime is about to collapse.

Women with a Strong Will

Next to the negative men, there are women who endure the hardship caused by the men. Some of them do not continue to endure it. At least two of them, Utako and Shizue, take action with their own willpower and change their environment. I adopted the words, "women with a strong will" from *Mukashibanashi to Nihonjin no Kokoro* [Folktales and Japanese Mind] (1982) by Hayao Kawai. The author is a Jungian psychologist. He examines the images of women in Japanese folktales to investigate the self-consciousness of Japanese women. Two of the images of femininity in the book reminded me of Utako and Shizue. Under the protection of her overprotective father,

Utako has been like a doll without her will. However, after she has been kidnapped by the motorcycle gang and the environment has been changed, she becomes the leader of the group which her father despises. It is obvious from Ai's admirations of Utako's dignified beauty that it is the way of living that fits to Utako's nature. Utako, who has recognized her own nature and comes to life, is another version of "a wife who does not eat" in a Japanese folktale who runs away from her husband into the mountains, the fact being revealed that she has a big, hidden mouth on her head—which eats a lot (41-69).

Shizue reminds me of "a Charcoal-maker's wife." The wife, having endured her husband's absurdity and selfishness, runs out of patience and decisively runs away from him. She attains a happy life in another land. Shizue also leaves Mr. Kinoshita, a man who despises women, and becomes independent as a poet. Later he attends her book-signing, but runs away embarrassed by her success. This development is the same as that in "a Charcoal-maker's wife." The ex-husband of the wife has become a poor peddler and comes to her house without knowing that it is his ex-wife's house. She accepts him kindly, and he felt deeply ashamed of his foolishness and later dies (278-87). It is clear from the list of his favorite books in his essay, *Aku to Itansha* [Evil and a Heretic] (1995), that Yasutaka Tsutsui has read *Folktales and Japanese Mind*. They know each other well.

Anima and New Women

Next, I will examine the protagonist, Ai. For the author, Yasutaka Tsutsui, Ai might be Anima, "the opposite sex in a man's mind" in Jungian psychology. According to Jung's *Psychological Types*, which is in the list of Tsutsui's favorite books, in a man's mind there is a woman type (a man type in a woman's mind). Anima is one of the dwellers in the unconscious world, and the internal image of the opposite sex has a strong power on the creative activity of writers. It is translated as "spirit," or it is said to be a guide in the unconscious. Negative men might be the men who have lost Anima, a woman in his mind.

Yasutaka Tsutsui is a prolific writer. Among his stories featuring girls or young women, *Edipusu no Koibito* [Oedipus's Love] (1977) attracted me. It is the last volume of the series in which the main character is a girl, Nanase, who can see into other person's mind. (Ai also has a special capacity of understanding dog's language. The author seems to have a mystic image of Anima as possessing a supernatural power.) In this story Nanase has relationship with a handsome younger boy. His mother, Tamako, is a goddess (Ai's mother's name is also Tamako and this name is also the granddaughter's name in his *Watashi no Guranpa* [My Grandpa] [1999]). *Oedipus's Love* is science fiction, in which one day Tamako is suddenly chosen as a goddess and is entrusted the government of universe by an old god. The old god says to Nanase that the distortion in the long-lasting government by men has driven the earth to the brink of destruction and that it is morals peculiar to women that will rescue the earth from this predicament and that for that purpose this world is shifting to the government by a goddess. Although this goddess is an being that has been chosen, this is an image of a new woman which surpasses the scale of "a woman with strong will." The author believes that the regime should be shifted from being male-dominated to female-dominated for humans to survive on this earth and he has a goddess symbolize a woman who will govern the regime. It is surprising that this science fiction writer insisted thirty-six years ago that the competitive society supported by men should be replaced by the cooperative society that women wish for. In *Ai's Left Side*, this image of a goddess might be put into the girl protagonist. Utilizing her experiences in her journey as a textbook, Ai learns various patterns of negative men, and being supported by the old man's lessens, she looks through their true nature, and in the end she attains a capacity to judge the degree of their evil. She exercises this capacity most dramatically on her father. It might be because a father symbolizes the old male-dominated regime.

All that a girl needs to do when she grows up to be "a new woman" is learning, because it is wise women's power that will save the future of the earth. *Ai's Left Side* is the story in which the author brings up his Anima to be "a new woman."

This story is a warning to the negative men who have lost their Animas and an encouragement to the women who endeavor to grow. At the same time, it includes a message that education is essential for children.

The reason Ai sowed seeds of conflict between two male characters might be that they have abandoned their most significant role of educating children. By telling her father that her mother's employer stole her money, Ai intends to make them quarrel and ruin themselves.

This attitude of Ai's which looks coldhearted should not be judged based on the old moral. Considering that this story regards adults' negligence of children's education and their independence as the greatest evil, Ai's breaking off relations with her father is necessary for the girl's independence.

At first, I felt extremely satisfied with the severance of the relations with the hateful negative men, but later I realized that Ai's revenge was not personal, but it was to accelerate independence of women in general.

II. The Ability of Severance and the Future

What Is the Ability of Severance?

The time of this story seems to be a near future, but it also seems to be a turbulent period in an age ago. The desperate situation that could not be broken through with makeshift efforts or devices is prevailing. However, this anarchy makes the adventure story possible. What is "the ability of severance" which the protagonist has attained in this situation?

We exercise "the ability of severance" in our everyday life: We decisively cut our hair short, cut off the overgrown branches of the trees in our yard, or cast away the unnecessary things we have long preserved and not given up. Or we refuse requests, judging that it exceeds our ability even if we are expected to do it, or we break off contact with a person whom we do not get on well with. In other words, "the ability of severance" is the power to go on forward, breaking out of the trapped situation or a standstill.

The Ability of Severance and the Direction

Ai, however, exercises the ability of severance in a bigger scale than these, which symbolizes the severance that stakes women's independence. Ai severs relations rather with a father in general, a father with old values and who lives in the male-dominated regime, not just with Ai's personal father. Why is such a serious role assigned to Ai? I examined the four women in the story.

Ai's mother, Tamako Tsukioka, has a capacity to support herself while raising children. She knows that she should support her husband, but she is not able to look through the negative aspects of her husband and break off the relations with him. Shizue, some years younger than Tamako, observing her position objectively, is able to express herself in poetry and criticize the negative man, but she has no capacity to support herself economically and the execution of her ability of severance is suspended. Utako, two years older than Ai, being hurt by the sudden change in environment, her potential is awakened and acted like a hero in the turbulent times, using the power without any restraint. Her power of severance is very strong, and it functions in every direction to shake off difficulties, and, in an occasion, she does not mind killing. Although both Shizue and Utako are women with a strong will, the directions of their exercises are different. This difference might cause the difference in their future. While Shizue has an opportunity to survive as an excellent poet, in accordance with her efforts, Utako has a possibility to become a criminal in the peaceful time which will come after the turbulent period. Utako would have to pay a big price for having displayed her ability regardless of the directions. In other words, the ability of severance needed by women will not last long or be temporary if the direction is not appropriate, or if the severance is not connected to human growth.

A fifteen-year-old girl, Ai, has just gained the ability of severance. The direction to use it is not yet decided. It is said that the girls around these ages, in adolescence, become very sensitive to their father's negative aspects. At this age, I remember I myself took the most defiant attitudes toward my father. Adolescence is the time when we destroy the old self and create a new self, that is to say, the time between a child and an adult. In such an unstable situation, the girls desperately search for trustworthy values. At such a time, girls resist against their fathers' old values, selfishness, deception and unfairness. In some occasions, they do not avoid severance of the relations with their fathers to protect themselves from their bad influences. The reason girls' power of severance is sharper and more merciless than older women's is that it is their matter of life and death.

The purpose in Ai's going to university is not to gain an academic record but to learn about the wide world and complexity of human beings. The goddess who governs the new world needs to know about the world by learning various things and to find the right direction and the effects of her ability of severance. The reason that the author chose a girl among the four women might be that girls have the longest time in the future and the biggest capacity to learn about the unknown world and take in what they have learned.

A Girl Inside Me

I feel that a girl who resembles Ai, a protagonist with an unyielding spirit, lives inside me. Although my father is my blood relation, for a long time he and I have not understood each other, and he has been, so to speak, just a shape of my left arm which is dysfunctional. However, when I read this book, which approves the girl's ability of severance, I felt that I may be permitted to sever relations with my father, but what is to be severed is not my father as an individual, but the negative aspects in my father as a man. This discovery provided me with a split in the trapped situation of the distrust of men.

Although I have strongly wished to trust people, actually I have excluded men from the objectives. However, I wish there be the both sexes in this split in my future.

The Ability of Severance

The ability of severance is the ability to break up the impasse which the person has long suffered and to urge him or her to step forward. If the direction aims at growth, it will make the future wide and bright.

Appendix: *Ai's Left Side* (Summary)

This is a near-future novel relating the time in which an old system governed by men is collapsing. Ai is a beautiful and bright girl aged twelve. One day she runs away from the store at Hagi-cho, where she has lived, heading for Tokyo. The purpose is to look for her father, who has suddenly disappeared, abandoning Ai and her mother, who have had no contact from him. The watch-dog, Great Dane, is attending Ai on her left side. It is guarding Ai in return for her mother's kindness to it. For some reason Ai can communicate with dogs.

During the three years when she fights against enemies such as the pursuer sent by the shopkeeper, motorcycle gangs who try to rob her money and a man with Lolita complex, she meets an old man and is educated by him. The first love with one of her classmates and the rescue of the women whose independence is interrupted by men—these experiences enforce her ability to discern the evil of society and to avoid it.

In the end, she confronts her father. Disillusioned by his indecency, greediness and cunning, she severs the father-and-daughter relationship. Ai, who now does not need a guardian, has become independent, as a supporter of a new society governed by women.

Works Consulted

Jung, C.G. *Psychological Types*. Princeton: Princeton UP, 1971. Vol. 6 of *The Collected Works of C.G. Jung*. Trans. R. F. C. Hull. 20 vols. 1970-1979.

Kawai, Hayao 河合隼雄. *Mukashibanashi to Nihonjin no Kokoro* [Folktales and Japanese Mind] 昔話と日本人の心. Tokyo: Iwanami Shoten 岩波書店, 1982.

Storr, Anthony. *Yungu* ユング. Trans. Kawai Hayao 河合隼雄. Tokyo: Iwanami Shoten 岩波書店, 1978. Trans. of *C.G. Jung*. New York: Viking Press, 1973.

Tsutsui, Yasutaka 筒井康隆. *Ai no Hidarigawa* [Ai's Left Side] 愛のひだりがわ. Tokyo: Iwanami Shoten 岩波書店, 2002.

---. *Aku to Itansha* [Evil and a Heretic] 悪と異端者. Tokyo: Chuo Koronsha 中央公論社, 1995.

---. *Edipusu no Koibito* [Oedipus's Love] エディプスの恋人. Tokyo: Shinchosha 新潮社, 1977.

---. *Watashi no Guranpa* [My Grandpa] わたしのグランパ. Tokyo: Bungei Shunju 文藝春秋, 1999.

Yamanaka, Yasuhiro 山中康裕. *Ehon to Dowa no Yungu Shinrigaku* [Picture Books and Stories for Children in the Light of Jungian Psychology] 絵本と童話のユング心理学. 1986. Tokyo: Chikuma Shobo 筑摩書房, 1997.

Chapter X

In the Garden of Integration and Restoration
—What Is the Significance of
The Secret Garden to Burnett?—

Frances Hodgson Burnett
The Secret Garden

New York: Frederick A. Stokes; London: William Heinemann, 1911

* Japanese edition: Burnett, Frances Hodgson. *Himitsu no Hanazono*. Trans. Reiko Yamanouchi. Illus. Shirley Hughes. Tokyo: Iwanami Shoten, 2005.

I. Into the Mother's Garden

The "Fairy Tale" as the Model

Burnett is said to have been a great reader. I do not know what books she read, but it is said that she loved fairy tales and was an imaginative girl who wished to be "a fairy godmother" (Nyu Fantaji no Kai 26, 84). The period during which she had great success is considered the Golden Age of children's literature in Britain and America (from the first half of the nineteenth century to the latter half of the twentieth century). Burnett and J. M. Barrie, who wrote *Peter Pan*, were both successful British novelists, Barrie being eleven years older than Burnett. Their works were dramatized and repeatedly staged in London and New York.

Burnett's *The Secret Garden* was published simultaneously in Britain and

America, five years later than Barrie's *Peter Pan in Kensington Gardens*. They almost certainly were aware of each other's works. From reading *Peter Pan in Kensington Gardens* I was able to find some answers for the questions I had in reading *The Secret Garden*. This experience led me to think that Burnett's *The Secret Garden* had been written with *Peter Pan in Kensington Gardens* as its model. This comparison of these two novels is hinted by the coincidence that H. Carpenter's essays in criticism, *Secret Gardens: A Study of the Golden Age of Children's Literature*, which is the same title as Burnett's, which I read as a reference book, dealt with these two works. *The Secret Garden* by Burnett is a story about an orphaned girl, Mary, who is taken in by her uncle and forced to move from her home in India to his mansion in England. She discovers a secret garden, guided by a robin. She revives the deserted garden together with a boy, Dickon, and her cousin, Colin, who recovers eventually from a long-term illness.

I had three questions: the first one is the relationships between the robin and humans.

- In the scene where a robin comes near to Mary without hesitation:
  Oh, to think that he should actually let her come as near to him as that! He knew nothing in the world would make her put out her hand toward him or startle him in the least tiniest way. He knew it because he was a real person. . . . (F. Burnett, *The Secret Garden* 57, emphasis mine)

Yoko Inokuma translated it as "The robin is a real person" literally. What does it mean to call a robin "a real person"? Although this story is more or less fantastic, it is a realistic novel. I was amazed by Inokuma's bold translation. The other translators, Tomoko Nakayama and Reiko Yamanouchi, translated this part as "It seemed to be a real person." Inokuma translated in other parts in the same way as the other translators. However, such a bold translation in which a robin is considered to be a real person gives the readers a strong impression, possibly exceeding the translator's intention.

The second question is why it is necessary to refer to a missel thrush. The old gardener, Ben, whose only friend has been the robin before Mary appears, says to Mary that she is like a robin because she has quickly become very close to him. Mary and Dickon, who helps Ben with his gardening and is a child of nature, or a bird, are both like robins to Ben, but Dickon says Mary is a missel thrush, who endeavors to guard her nest (the garden she has discovered).

I wondered why Mary is compared to a missel thrush. Whereas the robin acts an important role from the beginning to the end, the missel thrush is used as a metaphor by the children only in the middle of the story. What is the reason for that?

I will extract from the book the scenes where the missel thrush is referred to.

- The scene where Dickon reassures Mary, who wants to keep the existence of the garden secret:

    'If tha' was a missel thrush an' showed me where they nest was, does tha' think I'd tell anyone? Not me,' . . . . 'Tha' art as safe as a missel thrush.' (88)

- The scene where Mary, after finishing lunch, hurries back to the garden and finds a picture Dickon has left:

    Then she saw it was meant for a nest with a bird sitting on it. (96)

- The scene where a housemaid, Martha, looks at her brother, Dickon's picture:

    Martha said, 'There's a picture of a missel thrush on her nest. . . .'

    [. . .]

    Then Mary knew Dickon had meant the picture to be a message. He had meant that she might be sure he would keep her secret. <u>Her garden was her nest and she was like a missel thrush</u>. (96, emphasis mine)

- The scene where Colin is informed of the existence of the garden, Mary becomes nervous:
  > Everything would be spoiled—everything. Dickon would never come back. She would never again feel <u>like a missel thrush with a safe hidden nest</u>. (103, emphasis mine)

- The scene where Colin continues to ask about the garden persistently and Mary explains about the significance of keeping it secret:
  > 'You see—you see . . . if no one knows but ourselves . . . —and we could find it; . . . and <u>we called it our garden</u> and pretended that— that <u>we were missel thrushes and it was our nest</u>, and if we played there almost every day and dug and planted seeds and made it all come alive—' (103, emphasis mine)

I perceive from these phrases that the missel thrush's nest to Mary is a safe and secret place that she found at first only for her sake, but then, unexpectedly, it is easily disclosed to Dickon, who can understand a robin's words. This disclosure is much easier than to Colin. Then, Mary grants her cousin, Colin, permission to enter the garden, and it becomes the place for the three to work together.

The third question is why Colin talks to Mary about the golden trumpets in a book when Colin opens the window and gets excited with the spring breeze blowing in. Although the book which Colin talks about cannot be identified, there might be a model.

In searching for the model I will quote the passages in *Peter Pan in Kensington Gardens* (1906), by J. M. Barrie.

- birds = children

> All children could have such recollections if they would press their hands hard to their temples, for, having been birds before they were human.... (30)

> They came out of the eggs daily, and laughed at him at once; then off they soon flew to be humans.... (44)

- Dickon is a fairy, Colin is a human, and Peter Pan is "Betwixt-and-Between."

> Peter's heart was so glad that he felt he must sing all day long, just as the birds sing for joy, but, being partly human, he needed an instrument, so he made a pipe of reeds . . . and played them so beautifully that even the birds were deceived.... (46-47)

- A thrush's nest holds water.

There is a chapter titled "The Thrush's Nest" in *Peter Pan in Kensington Gardens*. I will quote some passages from it:

> . . . they [Peter and Solomon] called a meeting of the thrushes. You will see presently why thrushes only were invited.
> . . . . He [Solomon] began by saying that he had been much impressed. . . . Other birds, said Solomon, omitted to line their nests. . . .
> "Consider," he said at last, "how warm the mud makes the nest." (59-61)

> Solomon said their young friend, Peter Pan, as they well knew, wanted very much to be able to cross to the Gardens, and he now proposed, with their help, to build a boat. (62)

> Solomon explained . . . the proposed boat was to be simply a thrush's nest large enough to hold Peter. (63)

The feature of a thrush's nest is that it holds water. What Dickon intends to convey to Mary by the picture of a thrush's nest might be that he will never leak her secret to anyone and make her feel reassured. He might intend to compare Mary's situation to a thrush's nest, rather than Mary to a thrush.

- ■ The trumpets bray at the fairy wedding.

The Queen of the fairies, who can be compared to Colin's mother, has a vassal, a duke, who is an oriental fairy. He is enfeebled from a dreadful disease, namely the inability to love. He might be compared to Colin, who is modeled after an Indian raja. It is Brownie, an ugly maid singer that cures his disease. She might be compared to Mary.

At the fairy wedding, the trumpets bray and a thousand couples dance in wild abandon in the spring (147). On the other hand, Colin, in the morning when he goes out to enter the garden, breathes the fresh spring air coming from the window, and remembers a book in which to the sound of the golden trumpets a crowd of happy people and children dance and blow pipes. This book might refer to the fairy tale, *Peter Pan in Kensington Gardens*. A number of other examples of correspondence can be found.

In Kensington Gardens there is a chimney sweeper, whose name is "Sooty." It means smoke-stained. The name reminds me of that of the crow which is Dickon's pet, "Soot." The hero, Peter Pan, plays a pipe and keeps a goat like Dickon.

Thus, I have examined the three questions. In examining them, I came to believe that Burnett was strongly moved by Barrie's work and created a story which led to the diverse direction. Whereas *Peter Pan in Kensington Gardens* by Barrie is, summarized simply, a story of a boy who has been shut out of the window by his mother, Burnett's *The Secret Garden* might be summarized as a story of a mother who embraces again her son who believes he is shut out by his mother.

In this essay, I would like to examine the reason Burnett felt driven to write such a story, in other words, what is the significance of this story to the author.

II. Belief in Fairies as Guardian Spirits and Christian Science

Belief in Fairies as Guardian Spirits

H. Carpenter, a British critic, points out that in the Golden Age of British children's literature (from the 1860s to the 1930s, according to his classification) literary men of this age longed for a spiritual and symbolic core that would take the place of the Christian God (*Secret* 13). He illustrates it with the fact that after the theatrical performance of Barrie's *Peter Pan* became a great success, fairies filled the children's books and the phenomena seemed to be almost a religious belief[1] (qtd. in Carpenter, *Secret* 180-81). Judging from the correspondence of the two stories that I have mentioned, I believe that *The Secret Garden* is a genuine fairy tale dressed in realism. Dickon, a child of nature, is similar to Peter Pan and he might be a spirit of a robin who knows everything. Mary might also be a robin unconsciously. In this story, a belief in fairies as guardian spirits who will protect humans in the real world lies in the background. And the robin is a messenger of its mother, a fairy godmother, that is, Lilias, Colin's mother.

Thus, Burnett loved and tried to believe in fairies, spiritual beings. This attitude is presented in the episode that she wrote *The Secret Garden*, initially inspired by a robin that flew to her garden. Gardening was one of her great loves. I have mentioned that the story of *The Secret Garden* might be a mirror image of the story of *Peter Pan in Kensington Gardens* from a mother's viewpoint. It might suggest that Burnett herself suffered from a lot of anxieties and was distressed with her way of living and earnestly desired to solve the problems.

Christian Science

As is known well, Burnett had two sons. The elder son, Lionel, who was fifteen years old, died from progressive tuberculosis when Burnett was forty years old. She was a popular writer and left the care for her children to a black nursemaid. Burnett worked like a manuscript-producing machine. She traveled a lot and traveled between home in the U.S. and her birth place Britain as many as 30 times. She, as a mother, might have felt terribly guilty about her son. Partly because of this sense of guilt and partly because of overwork, she began to suffer from neurasthenia, or depression, around the age of thirty-three (Nyu Fantaji no Kai 20, 40, 42, 44, 46, 49, 61-62, 66, 126-27).

One of the remedies that cured her was treatment based upon her religious belief. When she was about thirty-five, she encountered Christian Science, which was a kind of a psychotherapeutic system originating from Christianity (Nyu Fantaji no Kai 126-27). The founder, Mary Baker Eddy was weak ever since her childhood and studied the Bible by herself. She began to preach that sickness was only an illusion and humans were healed by perceiving the presence of God more intensely ("Meri").

Christian Science was popular with the wealthy classes. It was the religious group founded by Mary Baker in Boston in America in 1879. It denied original sin. She argued that God, who was generally considered to be a paternal existence, had both paternity and maternity and that human nature was spiritual. The practice based upon psychotherapy attracted the comparatively wealthy and progressive classes. She developed a psychotherapeutic system based on the principle that the reality is only spiritual and that the material and the materialistic senses (sin, sickness death and etc.) are only illusions. Her religious teaching spread with the texts, *Science and Health with Key to the Scriptures* (1875) and *Manual of The Mother Church* (1895). The headquarters are in Boston. The mass is practiced mainly by reading the Bible and her books and singing the hymns. It is famous for publishing an influential newspaper, *The Christian Science Monitor* (1908–) (Gakken Henshubu 214).

The noteworthy points in this doctrine are that it denies original sin which is generally believed to be in every human and that God is hermaphrodite and maternity is added to God. I perceive the similarity between this maternity and the characteristics of godmother bestowed to fairies in Burnett's works.

This consideration leads me to believe that Burnett tried to restore herself as a mother or a woman in *The Secret Garden* by re-tying the relationships between the mother inside herself and her son. In the conversation and the behavior of Collin and Mary this belief seems to be strongly expressed.

> 'Mrs. Craven was a very lovely young lady,' he had gone on rather hesitatingly. 'An' mother she thinks maybe she's about Misselthwaite many a time lookin' after Mester Colin, same as all mothers do when they're took out o' th' world. They have to come back, tha' sees. Happen she's been in the garden an' happen it was her set us to work, an' told us to bring him here.' (164)

This nature of a godmother is related to Christian Science. Burnett became a follower when her son, Lionel, was ten years old (the Colin character is the same age) and it is known that she had devoted herself to this belief by the age of fifty-nine, when she began to write *The Secret Garden* (Nyu Fantaji no Kai 52, 126). This story, however, was not written to disseminate the idea. In Burnett's story the door to the mother's garden is opened wide to rescue all the people, and in the background there is the world of fairies hidden with the fairy godmother in the middle of them.

III. Integration and Restoration

Burnett, Who Had to Live as a Head of a Family
The Secret Garden is like an overgrown giant tree with boughs and twigs

entangled intricately. It is a multilayered creation which admits various interpretations by readers. The girlish title had alienated me from reading it for a long time, but the first reading gave me an impression that this is the story of the restoration of the head of a family. The reason is that at the end of the story the head of the family and his son embark on a shared life in the family home. Among a lot of versions of digests and translations, I read a translation by Kazue Shinkawa, a poet. Then I read three translations by Reiko Yamanouchi, Tomoko Nakayama and Yoko Inokuma. In spite of that, my first impression did not change. I thought that the fact that Burnett wrote *The Head of the House of Coombe* two years before her death might support my first impression in reading *The Secret Garden*.

The reason Burnett continued to be interested in the theme until her later years might be that she had to be the head of the house although she was a woman and *The Secret Garden* might have been written to recover her womanliness.

In the postscript to the book (in Iwanami Library for young people, 2005) by the translator, Reiko Yamanouchi, Burnett's life is introduced with her biography by Ann Thwaite (1932–). I will summarize it here.

* * *

Burnett lived an eventful life full of glories and disappointments. She was born in Manchester, England in 1849. Her father, who was a merchant, died when she was three years old. In 1865, she moved to live in America, a new world, with her mother and four siblings, expecting to be supported by her uncle. Three years later, she earned thirty-five dollars, which was a big money at that time. Her contribution sent to a publisher had been accepted. This money supported her family completely. After that, she continued to write fifty or more novels and plays and more than sixty short-stories or essays until seventy-four, when she died. It was Burnett, not her husband who supported the family budget even after they married.

In the 1870s and the 1880s, Burnett was said to be one of the most important writers in America and Britain. However, in her glorious success as a writer, she was exposed to the curious eyes of the world and mass media. In those days, it was normal for women to stay at home. She failed in marriage twice, lost a son to illness and she herself suffered from repeated illness (Thwaite).

* * *

Although she was good at writing from her childhood, the exhaustion and stress from overloading work must have been excessive. It can be imagined that she might have wanted to escape from everything. Adding to that, she lost her son. This state of mind might be compared to Craven's, the head of Misselthwaite in *The Secret Garden*. Both are the head of the family in despair. I find correspondences between *The Secret Garden* and her life: India to Britain in the days of imperialism, Britain to America, a new world, and Yorkshire dialect to American English.

Naturalization as an American
She became an American citizen in 1905, when her ex-husband, Swan, died (Nyu Fantaji no Kai 74). She had been in America for eight years when she married Swan, so she had qualified for citizenship then, but she did not naturalize until she had lived in the United States for forty years. The reason might be that her longings for England were too intense to do so earlier. However, it was America that she chose at last. She wrote *The Secret Garden* as an American writer.

On the contrary, a contemporary writer, Henry James (1843–1926), was an American who took British citizenship.

A Japanese writer, Saiichi Maruya makes the protagonist in his novel, *Kagayaku Hi no Miya* [Lady of the Shining Sun] (2003) say that James's interest in ghosts originated from his fascination with the past, and he became British because there is no past in America (207-08). If America can be termed a place with no past, we could say that it took forty years for

Burnett to fully accept the land of future (America) as her "home."

The Dialogues between the Parts of Burnett's Personality

What I find the most interesting and valuable in *The Secret Garden* is the quarrels or battles with words between a little perverse Mary and very perverse Colin. As the saying goes, it is like the pot calling the kettle black. Their talks generated from their true and honest feelings sweep away the webs of the spiders that dwell in the old English mansion that had survived for more than six hundred years, and they are so exhilarating that the readers' stress is blown away. Mary is appalled at Colin, who is effeminate and piteous, frightened by death without reason. She uses strong words about Colin's selfishness. On the other hand, Colin gets furious at Mary's pitiless and undisguised words, and exposes all the wounds inside his mind which he was not able to confide to anyone. He, a ten-year-old boy, says that he is weak and his back will crook like his father's and he will die sooner or later, that he is resentful of his mother who died in an accident in the garden leaving him as a baby as well as of his father, who, having failed to overcome his wife's death, hates him.

Colin might be equivalent to Burnett's elder son, Lionel, and at the same time, he is the author's weakened heart. In the process of writing, Burnett might have descended to the bottom of her heart and became the girl Mary, and only by doing so, she might be able to talk to his son on an equal basis. This was an adventure which did not allow failure, but to recover herself she might have to confront the wound of her soul and make the parts of her personality fight against each other and listen to what they had to say.

Disappearance of Mary

Removing the dressing of realism, Mary and Dickon would be robins. When their roll has been fulfilled, the reason for them to be there is lost. They have to go back to where they should be, home. In the story the home is a fairyland that Lilias rules. The imbalance of the structure of *The Secret Garden* has been pointed out as the protagonist, Mary, loses her presence in the end of the story. However, it can be understood if they are considered to be fairies, not humans.

I have explained that a fairy tale lies behind this story in Section I. Now I will examine the meaning of Mary's disappearance, regarding it as a work of realism.

Burnett achieved success socially, standing on a par with men, which was rather a rare case at the time. However, on the contrary, she was not able to be successful in being a woman. She might have intended to heal herself in the mother's garden (in Lilias's garden or by godmotherliness of Christian Science). It might be expressed by Mary's behavior in which she tries to protect a small nest. Mary's power of action takes the author's depressed soul (= Colin) out into a bright garden. Mary is endowed with womanliness. The reason Mary is not in the last scene might be that Mary's womanliness is absorbed by Colin's manliness. That is to say, the parts of the author's characteristics are integrated. This last scene seems to be a proper grand final.

I have found that in *The Secret Garden* Burnett started from Christianity in England, took in fairy tales, and opened the door to Christian Science, a new thought established in America.

In contemplating Burnett's life I have found that a human proceeds after all to what he or she wants to be. Life is a series of unexpected events and we seem to spend all our time coping with them, but what we once longed for never disappears and while it sinks in the bottom of our minds, it becomes a compass of our behavior. It was a door in her mind that Burnett, who had longed for "a fairy godmother" in her childhood, opened for the last time.

The Secret Garden for Burnett is the story in which she tried to restore another side of herself—a side which she had not been able to live.

Note

1. Avery, Gillian. "The Quest for Fairyland." *The Quarterly Journal of the Library of Congress* 38. 4 (Fall 1981): 226.

Works Consulted

Barrie, J. M. *Peter Pan in Kensington Gardens*. London: Hodder & Stoughton, 1906. New York: Dover, 2008.
Burnett, Frances Hodgson. *The Secret Garden*. Ware: Wordsworth Editions, 1993.
Burnett, Vivian. *The Romantic Lady (Frances Hodgson Burnett): The Life Story of an Imagination*. New York: Scribner's, 1927.
Carpenter, Humphrey. *Secret Gardens: A Study of the Golden Age of Children's Literature*. 1985. London: Faber & Faber, 2009.
---. *Himitsu no Hanazono: Eibei Jido Bungaku no Ogon Jidai* [Secret Gardens: A Study of the Golden Age of Children's Literature] 秘密の花園：英米児童文学の黄金時代. Trans. Sadamatsu Tadashi 定松正. Tokyo: Kobian Shobo こびあん書房, 1988.
Gakken Henshubu 学研編集部, ed. *Kirisutokyo no Hon: Seibo, Tenshi, Seijin to Zenshuha no Girei* [The Book of Christianity: The Holy Mother, Angels, Saints and the Rituals of All the Religious Sects] キリスト教の本：聖母・天使・聖人と全宗派の儀礼. Vol. 2. Tokyo: Gakushu Kenkyusha 学習研究社, 1996. 2 vols.
Inokuma, Yoko 猪熊葉子, trans. *Himitsu no Hanazono* [The Secret Garden] 秘密の花園. By Frances Hodgson Burnett. Tokyo: Fukuinkan Shoten 福音館書店, 1979.
Maruya, Saiichi 丸谷才一. *Kagayaku Hi no Miya* [Lady of the Shining Sun] 輝く日の宮. Tokyo: Kodansha 講談社, 2003.
"Meri Beka Edei" [Mary Baker Eddy] メリー・ベーカー・エディ. *Wikipedia* ウィキペディア. 25 July 2016 <https://ja.wikipedia.org/wiki/メリー・ベーカー・エディ>.
Miyake, Okiko 三宅興子. "Himitsu no Hanazono Ron" [An Essay on *The Secret*

Garden]『秘密の花園』論. *Eibei Jido Bungaku Gaido: Sakuhin to Riron* [A Guide to British and American Literature for Children: The Works and the Theories] 英米児童文学ガイド：作品と理論. Ed. Nihon Igirisu Jido Bungaku-kai [Japanese Society for Children's Literature in English] 日本イギリス児童文学会. Tokyo: Kenkyusha Shuppan 研究社出版, 2001. 93-101.

Nakayama, Tomoko 中山知子, trans. *Himitsu no Hanazono* [The Secret Garden] 秘密の花園. By Frances Hodgson Burnett. Tokyo: Kodansha 講談社, 1991.

Nyu Fantaji no Kai ニューファンタジーの会. *Yume no Kariudo: Furanshisu Eichi Banetto no Sekai* [A Dream Hunter: The World of Frances H. Burnett] 夢の狩り人：Frances H. Burnettの世界. Tokyo: Todosha 透土社, 1994.

Paul, Lissa. "Enigma Variations: What Feminist Theory Knows about Children's Literature." *Children's Literature: The Development of Criticism.* Ed. Peter Hunt. London: Routledge, 1990. 148-65.

Shinkawa, Kazue 新川和江, trans. *Himitsu no Hanazono* [The Secret Garden] ひみつの花園. By Frances Hodgson Burnett. Tokyo: Kaiseisha 偕成社, 1972.

Thwaite, Ann *Waiting for the Party: The Life of Frances Hodgson Burnett, 1849–1924.* New York: Scribner's, 1974.

Yamanouchi, Reiko 山内玲子, trans. *Himitsu no Hanazono* [The Secret Garden] 秘密の花園. By Frances Hodgson Burnett. Tokyo: Iwanami Shoten 岩波書店, 2005.

Chapter XI

The Two in the Haze
—Why was *Peter Pan* Born?—

J. M. Barrie
Peter and Wendy

Illustrated by F. D. Bedford

London: Hodder & Stoughton; New York: Scribner's, 1911

* Japanese edition: Barrie, J. M. *Pita Pan to Wendi*. Trans. Momoko Ishii. Tokyo: Fukuinkan Shoten, 1972.

I. Encountering and Pursuing *Peter Pan*

For a long time *Peter Pan* was to me only the hero in the Walt Disney movie. However, when I read a complete translation, I found that Peter Pan was "an eternal boy" who was created by a famous dramatist, J. M. Barrie (1860–1937), in the Victorian and Georgian eras, and that he still fascinates both adults and children.

There are three versions of *Peter Pan* that feature this hero. Shigetoshi Suzuki, who is a researcher of Barrie and translated *The Little White Bird* (1902) describes:

#1—*Peter Pan in Kensington Gardens* (1906): A novel for adults.

#2—*Peter and Wendy* (1911): A novel for children. This is often called just *Peter Pan* after the copyright had expired.

#3—*Peter Pan; or, the Boy Who Wouldn't Grow Up* (1928): A play first staged in 1904 and published 24 year later.

These are related to each other and they all tell the story of Peter Pan, a boy who does not grow up.

Peter and Wendy was written in the later years of the golden age of British and American Children's literature. The critic, H. Carpenter, writes:
> Yet if little more need be said about the personal origins of *Peter Pan,* this still leaves us asking what there was in the play which touched such a crucial public nerve. Why did the private, half-mad dream of such a strange individual have such huge appeal to playgoers and readers? (*Secret* 176)

As an answer for these questions, Carpenter points out: the model of Peter Pan is the creator himself; he had a special talent to play various characters of people, being especially good at a boy who could not grow up; this boy, in the trilogy of *Peter Pan*, as a fascinating god for children, has an adventure in the fantastic world, and this, at the time of writing, satisfied people's desire for a new religion that would replace Christianity, and it formed a current in which fairy tales become pseudo-religion (*Secret* 170-87).

Carpenter's analysis is very persuasive. What interested me most was why Barrie created *Peter Pan*. I will pursue this theme in this essay.

There is a passage in *J. M. Barrie and the Lost Boys* (1979), Barrie's biography written by Andrew Birkin, which suggests Barrie's intention to write *Peter Pan*. Barrie writes to a leading actress:
> I have written a play for children, which I don't suppose would be much use in America. She [Wendy] is rather a dear of a girl with ever so many children long before her hair is up . . . . (103)

Barrie said to the promoter of the play, "I am sure it will not be a commercial success. But it is a dream-child of mine" (Birkin, *J. M. Barrie* 104).

These phrases suggest that Barrie was not confident about the play, *Peter Pan*, but what he was strongly attached to this work.

It is not widely known among general readers that, before Barrie wrote the trilogy of *Peter Pan*, he published a novel for adults, *The Little White Bird* in 1902. This has twenty-six chapters with more than three hundred pages, in which a boy with the image of Peter Pan appears for the first time. It took the author four years (1898–1902) to complete this book, a part of which became *Peter Pan in Kensington Gardens*. The boys who were models of Peter Pan and their family really existed, and the friendship between them and Barrie started in 1897, one year before he started writing this book (Birkin, *J. M. Barrie* 55).

II. *The Little White Bird* and *Peter and Wendy*

Here I will examine the relationships between *The Little White Bird* and *Peter and Wendy* to explore what Barrie intended to convey. First, I will introduce the summary of the story of *The Little White Bird*.

* * *

The narrator, I, Captain W, is a forty-seven-year-old bachelor. He is a novelist, who is an ex-serviceman. One day, W gets acquainted with a handsome boy, David, and becomes friends with him. In fact, W has known David's mother, Mary. She had been a live-in nurse six years before and was in love with her future husband. W happened to observe the couple's dating. He secretly helped them overcome hurdles in their relationship, and eventually reach marriage. That is to say, he played a part of Cupid. After that, he often rescued them from the difficulties in their life. W came to be respected by

Mary as an anonymous gentleman. When Mary was expecting a baby soon, W approached her husband and told a lie that W himself was in the same situation, that is, a husband whose wife is expecting. After a while, David was born to Mary. W said that his baby, Timothy (of course an imaginary son), had been born, but had died soon. He lied, driven into a corner. One year passed and when he sees David taking a walk with his nurse, he feels as if David is his own ideal son, Timothy. Having repeatedly been begged by Mary to meet him for four years, W meets her. Mary is a twenty-six-year-old mother. W dedicates to her *The Little White Bird* written by him and says that the story is about Mary and David, and that it is written for Mary. Then, Mary says that it is not true, but the story is about "the little white bird," that is, Timothy. W is confused by what Mary said, but he gradually realizes Mary is right. He is moved by her wisdom.

Next, I will introduce the summary of *Peter and Wendy*, referring to *Peter Pan in Kensington Gardens* and the play, *Peter Pan*, to complement the understanding of this work.

* * *

The time is the early 1900s, and the place is the three-storied building on the corner of a street in Bloomsbury in England, where the Darling family live. The head of the family, Mr. Darling, is a clerk in a downtown office. Mrs. Darling is a housewife and a mother of three children before school age. The eldest daughter, Wendy, supposedly seven years old, the eldest son, John, and the second son, Michael, have a nurse, a dog named Nana, and they have a maid. It is a typical middle-class family in England. However, they are not very wealthy, and Mr. Darling calculates the expense every time his wife gets pregnant to make sure whether they can afford its expense. It is beneficial for them to have a dog nurse because she does not claim a wage, but Mr. Darling is not satisfied with it because it is humiliating to have a dog nurse and Nana does not respect him.

One day, Mr. Darling loses his temper, caused by a trivial matter. He gets furious about their children being on Nana's side rather than on his, and he drives Nana away from the nursery into the backyard and ties her up. That night, while Mr. and Mrs. Darling are out, the three children fly away like birds out of the window lured by a boy, Peter Pan, toward Neverland (an imaginary place). Neverland is where lost boys who have fallen out of baby cars live with Peter, who is a master of Neverland. There, Wendy plays the role of mother to Peter, her young brothers and other nine lost boys at the underground house. Peter is supposed to be a father to the boys and a husband to Wendy, but it is just a pretension. Wendy, who wants to be Peter's girlfriend, is not satisfied with it, but Peter persists in dealing with Wendy as his mother. After having adventures with fairies, mermaids and Red Indians, Wendy becomes nostalgic for the days at home. Peter says to Wendy that mothers are not as trustworthy as children expect them to be and that having run away from home on the day he was born he had later returned and found his mother had forgotten him and she was with another child. However, Wendy persists in believing in her mother and goes back home with the other lost boys following her. On the way home, there is an adventure with pirates, and Peter and the children defeat Captain Hook. Peter arrives at the Darling's before Wendy does, and closes the window which Mrs. Darling has kept open, waiting for her children to come back. Peter does not want Wendy to return home. However, looking at tears on Mrs. Darling's cheeks and perceiving her affection to her children, Peter changes his mind. After the delightful reunion of the mother and her children, Peter and the lost children are asked to be the Darlings' children, but Peter refuses her offer and returns to Neverland.

For a long time Peter Pan had taken away girls to Neverland and had them play the role of mother and will continue to do so. The girls have been and will continue to be replaced, and only Peter continues to be an eternal boy—with infant teeth in a body which should be very old.

*   *   *

The structure of these two stories resembles each other. In both stories the hero is defeated by a young woman who has children: the novelist, W, who has a distorted love for Mary, is overwhelmed by Mary's cleverness, and on the other hand, Peter is defeated by Mrs. Darling's love for Wendy and returns alone to Neverland. This story can be read as that of a mother's love for children, but the reason why Peter is defeated easily by Mrs. Darling might be that she is a beautiful young woman even though he has a negative image for a mother.

In reading Barrie's biography we find that he strongly projects his own issues and experiences upon his plays and novels. He worked out elaborate works by replacing a protagonist's situation with another person's, or by changing the ages, and they became complicated. Barrie is said to have regarded literature as "games" (Honda 107). He took a massive amount of notes (Birkin, *J. M. Barrie* 31), and he always kneaded the ideas of his works into shape. He exerted his technical skills in writing.

Accordingly, it can be said that in writing *The Little White Bird* and *Peter and Wendy*, Barrie used various kinds of techniques although the former is a realism novel and the elaborateness in it is much less than in the latter, fantasy novel.

My first impression in reading *The Little White Bird* is that it is a collection of roundabout love letters from a novelist, W, to Mary. *Peter and Wendy* appears to be a story which depicts the love of Peter for Wendy. That is, both of these two stories are love stories.

In the tenth chapter in *The Little White Bird* there is a paragraph as follows:
> "They were all written to another woman, ma'am, and yet I am in hopes that you will find something in them about yourself." It would have sounded oddly to Mary, but life is gray to friendless girls, and something might have come of it.

On the other hand, it would have brought her for ever out of the wood of the little hut, and I had but to drop the letter to send them both back there. The easiness of it tempted me.

Besides, she would tire of me when I was really known to her. They all do, you see. (Chap. 10)

Although the novelist, W, says that his heart is broken by the lost love twenty years before, that Mary is under an illusion that she is loved by him and that he is not a right person to Mary, these are camouflages to the readers of his novels for his love of Mary, which is plainly discernible.

Thus, *The Little White Bird* was a technical love letter of a novelist devoted to a young woman, and *Peter and Wendy* might have been a stage where he could express freely his love to the young woman.

III. Barrie and Silvia

As I mentioned before, Barrie projected his own issues and experiences on his works. Reading these two works and his biography led me to agree with many of the readers and the critics in that the novelist, W, and the young woman in *The Little White Bird*, and Peter and Wendy in *Peter and Wendy* are Barrie and Silvia, the mother of the five boys whom Barrie befriended. In *Peter and Wendy*, Barrie changed himself and Silvia into a boy and a girl with his playful techniques. The reason might be that Barrie himself was, in a sense, a boy, and he turned Silvia into a girl as his companion. Peter is "an eternal boy," who never grows to be, wants to be nor can be an adult. This creation of the character might be related to his own situation. According to his biography, he was probably impotent and that could have been the cause of the discord with and divorce from his wife Mary, who was an actress. He did not hide his complex about his little body. He was "barely five foot," and even when he was older and wore beard, he had a childlike face. Although Barrie's longing for women was strong, women only considered him as a harmless person. However, he was loved by children and animals. He was a funny person to children. He made children laugh by telling funny things, moving his ears, and was also an enjoyable friend who loved to inspire children's imaginations (Birkin, *J. M. Barrie* 9-12, 31, 40-41, 180; Carpenter, *Secret* 173).

How did Silvia love Barrie?

To answer this question, it is necessary to know her background. I searched Barrie's biography for her family and her character (this works as a comparison between Silvia and her husband, Arthur). Arthur was the second son of a theologian famous for radical ideas. Her family was intellectual and full of vigor and rigidness. On the other hand, Silvia was a daughter of an artist and novelist who displayed his ability in drawing caricatures in *Punch* (a weekly magazine with pictures in Britain) for thirty years, so to speak, an artist. Silvia's mother felt misgivings about her daughter's fiancé because he was too rigid and inflexible, and too different from her daughter, who was cheerful and passionate. The families where Arthur and Silvia were brought up were too different (Birkin, *J. M. Barrie* 46-49).

Silvia was very creative and she loved beautiful things. Silvia, who seemed to have inherited her father's artistry although she did not write novels as her father or Barrie did, made by hand beautiful and unique clothing for her children and herself. A lot of photos of Silvia and her children in beautiful dresses remain, and what is the most striking is a red tam-o'-shanter (a big cap like a beret) made with strips cut from "an ancient judicial robe of red velvet that had once belonged to Arthur's grandfather" (Birkin, *J. M. Barrie* 54-55). We find echoes of Silvia's love of sewing in the fact that Peter Pan, who lives in another world, does not recognize the word, "kiss," as an expression of affection. He memorizes "thimble" as the word for that by mistake.

Five years before she met Barrie, Silvia had married handsome Arthur after a passionate courtship. Silvia was a good wife who loved her husband throughout her life, but she came to appreciate and rely on the comforts that wealthy

Barrie was able to offer her and the boys, a style of life beyond what a middle class husband could provide at that time (Birkin, *J. M. Barrie* 47-51).

This theme of how women of this era had to rely on the financial support of their husbands or society is expressed in Barrie's novels or plays.

> WENDY. Are none of the other children girls?
> PETER. Oh no; girls, you know, are much too clever to fall out of their prams.
> [. . .]
> PETER. I'll teach you how to jump on the wind's back and then away we go. . . . how we should all respect you. (*Peter Pan or The Boy Who Would Not Grow Up* ACT 1)

Hearing this, Wendy changes her mind.

The author mentions his former girlfriend:
> I told her what had been revealed to me as I looked upon her, and she trembled. . . .
> Because I knew the maid, she was mine. Every maid, I say, is for him who can know her. . . . I had . . . found the woman. (*The Little White Bird* Chap. 9)

> . . . until Wendy came her mother was the chief one. (*Peter Pan* 7)

> [When Wendy came] She wanted to risk it, come what might, but that was not his way. . . . (*Peter Pan* 9)

Mr. Darling desperately calculates the expenses for Wendy, and his wife appeals to her husband for generosity. This scene is repeated after the births of the next two children, but they decide to raise them after all. This means that the father who supports the economy of the family possesses the power to spare or take the lives of the children.

... and he was really the grander character of the two. (*Peter Pan* 9)

One of the lost boys, Nibs, says:
> NIBS. All I remember about my mother is that she often said to father, 'Oh how I wish I had a cheque book of my own.' (*Peter Pan or The Boy Who Would Not Grow Up* ACT 2)

Barrie, being a famous playwright, was able to give Silvia three things that women of this age wanted: love, understanding and wealth.

According to Barrie's biography, Silvia's husband, Arthur, recognized Barrie's harmlessness, and accepted his support, including his wealth (Birkin, *J. M. Barrie* 59, 144-45). Barrie was, for the Davies's, another generous father, who was like a nursemaid.

In *The Little White Bird*, the novelist, W, creates an imaginary son, Timothy, to make his story told to Mary's husband consistent. Timothy could be considered to be "the little white bird."

I was surprised to know that *Peter Pan* was the title chosen by the theatrical manager who changed it from the original title, "The Great White Father" (Birkin, *J. M. Barrie* 104-05). Barrie might have wanted to express his wish to be a father through creating Peter Pan although he was so old that no one can know his age.

The titles, *The Little White Bird* and *The Great White Father*, form a pair. This shows that these two are not separate but deeply connected. I conceive his intention of composition that Barrie's incarnation and Peter's forerunner, "the little white bird" named Timothy, becomes "the great white father" named Peter Pan.

IV. The Two in the Haze

I have looked at *The Little White Bird* and *Peter and Wendy* in connection with Barrie's love for Silvia. As these stories also involve issues of husbands and wives and children, these can be read from the viewpoints of men, women and children. That is why both adults and children feel empathy for these works, accepting them as their own stories. However, I believe that it is Barrie's technique, who regards writing as games. What Barrie hides by this multi-character viewpoint narrative style is the core theme of love for a young woman. It is hidden in the haze of technique and cannot be seen clearly.

There appear "a house in a dream" and "the hut in the pine wood haze" in *The Little White Bird* and, and "the little house" in *Peter and Wendy*.

> I had my delicious dream that night. I dreamt that I too was twenty-six, which was a long time ago, and that I took train to a place called my home, whose whereabouts I see not in my waking hours, and when I alighted at the station a dear lost love was waiting for me, and we went away together. (*The Little White Bird* Chap. 1)

> On the other hand, it would have brought her for ever out of the wood of the little hut, and I had but to drop the letter to send them both back there. (*The Little White Bird* Chap. 10)

> Everybody has heard of the Little House in the Kensington Gardens, which is the only house in the whole world that the fairies have built for humans. (*The Little White Bird* Chap. 17)

> My thoughts had reverted also, and for the last time my eyes saw the little hut through the pine wood haze. I met Mary there, and we came back to the present together. (*The Little White Bird* Chap. 26)

'But where are you going to live?'
'With Tink in the house we built for Wendy. . . .'
'How lovely,'. . . .
[. . .]
'Well then, come with me to the little house.' (*Peter Pan* 230)

"The house" and "the little hut" in *The Little White Bird* are the home in his dream for the writer and Mary, and "the little house" in *Peter Pan* is a home for Peter and Wendy as a pretend husband and wife. Although one is for children and the other for adults, both are Barrie's imaginary "lover's homes" that he was not able to obtain in his real life.

Barrie, at the beginning of *Peter Pan*, makes Mrs. Darling raise her voice filled with grief: [To her daughter] "Oh, why can't you remain like this for ever!" (7).

This is Mrs. Darling's lamentation over Wendy's growing-up, and this is also the grief for the fact that she herself has grown up.

When Wendy has grown up and got married, having almost forgotten about Peter, he comes back to see Wendy again. She wishes to return to her childhood. Thus, Wendy, like her mother, remembers her longing for Peter, whom she played with in her girlhood. The mother and the daughter are, in a sense, the same person, and Peter reminds Wendy's mother that she has seen him as a young boy by taking her daughter away with him.

Barrie's main purpose for writing this story is to liberate young women from adults and to take them to another world.

It was in Neverland haze that Barrie was able to love a young woman, Silvia, being a child liberated from his physical complex. For that purpose was *Peter Pan* created.

Works Consulted

Barrie, J. M. *The Little White Bird: or Adventures in Kensington Gardens.* London: Hodder & Stoughton, 1902. *Project Gutenberg.* 5 May 2016 <http://www.gutenberg.org/files/1376/1376-h/1376-h.htm>.

---. *Peter and Wendy.* London: Hodder & Stoughton; New York: Scribner's, 1911.

---. *Pita Pan to Wendi* [Peter and Wendy] ピーター・パンとウエンディ. Trans. Ishii Momoko 石井桃子. Tokyo: Fukuinkan Shoten 福音館書店, 1972.

---. *Peter Pan.* London: Hodder & Stoughton, 1928. London: Penguin Books, 2002.

---. *Peter Pan in Kensington Gardens.* London: Hodder & Stoughton, 1906. New York: Dover, 2008.

---. *Peter Pan or The Boy Who Would Not Grow Up. Project Gutenberg of Australia eBook.* 8 June 2016 <http://gutenberg.net.au/ebooks03/0300081h.html>.

Birkin, Andrew. *J. M. Barrie and the Lost Boys: The Real Story Behind Peter Pan.* London: Constable, 1979.

---. *Rosuto Boizu: J. M. Bari to Pita Pan Tanjo no Monogatari* [J. M. Barrie and the Lost Boys: The Real Story Behind Peter Pan] ロスト・ボーイズ：J. M. バリとピーター・パン誕生の物語. Trans. Suzuki Shigetoshi 鈴木重敏. Tokyo: Shinshokan 新書館, 1991.

Carpenter, Humphrey. *Secret Gardens: A Study of the Golden Age of Children's Literature.* 1985. London: Faber & Faber, 2009.

---. *Himitsu no Hanazono: Eibei Jido Bungaku no Ogon Jidai* [Secret Gardens: A Study of the Golden Age of Children's Literature] 秘密の花園：英米児童文学の黄金時代. Trans. Sadamatsu Tadashi 定松正. Tokyo: Kobian Shobo こびあん書房, 1988.

Honda, Akira 本多顕彰. Commentary. *Pita Pan* [Peter Pan] ピーター・パン. By J. M. Barrie. Trans. Honda. 1953. Tokyo: Shinchosha 新潮社, 1981. 107-08.

Kiley, Dan. *Pita Pan Shindoromu: Naze Karera wa Otona ni Narenainoka* ピーター・パン・シンドローム：なぜ、彼らは大人になれないのか. Trans. Okonogi Keigo 小此木啓吾. Tokyo: Shodensha 祥伝社, 1984. Trans. of *The Peter Pan Syndrome: Men Who Have Never Grown Up.* New York: Dodd, Mead, 1983.

Suzuki, Shigetoshi 鈴木重敏, trans. *Chisana Shiroi Tori* [The Little White Bird] 小さ

な白い鳥. By J. M. Barrie. Tokyo: Parorusha パロル舎, 2003.

Chapter XII

From an Incomprehensible Story to a Comprehensible Story
—*Tom's Midnight Garden* by Philippa Pearce—

Philippa Pearce
Tom's Midnight Garden

Illustrated by Susan Einzig

London: Oxford UP, 1958

* Japanese edition: Pearce, Philippa. *Tomu wa Mayonaka no Niwa de*. Trans. Ichiro Takasugi. Tokyo: Iwanami Shoten, 1967.

I. An Incomprehensible Story

Two Puzzling Scenes
Philippa Pearce's (1920–2006) books for children are very popular among Japanese readers. My favorites include *The Way to Sattin Shore* (1983), *A Dog So Small* (1962), *What the Neighbours Did and Other Stories* (1972), and *The Shadow-Cage and Other Tales of the Supernatural* (1977). What feature in these stories are fairies and ghosts who continue to dwell in the countryside or in old mansions, whom British people have cared for traditionally, rather than fictional places or characters. Roughly speaking, there is little absurdity in them, but they deal with mysterious experiences and incidents that we encounter in daily life.

However, her most valued work is *Tom's Midnight Garden*, published in 1958 and awarded in the same year the Carnegie Medal (a prize that The Library Association awards to an excellent children's literature). It is different from her other stories. J. R. Townsend, a famous British critic and writer of children's books, says that this is the masterpiece among children's books written after World War II (*Written* 128). The Japanese translator of this book, Ichiro Takasugi, admires it for its solid structure, comparing it to a beautiful work of architecture (340).

However, I was not able to appreciate its splendor, compared to other stories. The plot is very interesting, but I could not capture the structure of the time which flows in the story. I asked many people for their opinions, but they said they too could not capture it. Many of them were satisfied with the last scene in which the old woman and the boy embraced. It seems that they are not much concerned about the unaccountable matters, seemingly because the story is in a dream. To be honest, I do not accept the claimed high value of a work without understanding it. I made efforts to understand this work by reading several times, and I recognized that the reason for the high evaluation lays within two puzzling scenes, In the scenes, in the sixth and the twenty-seventh chapters, one scene is written as if it happened in a different time. In this essay, I will make the interpretation of this scene a key to search the structure of this story and the author's intention.

I will quote the two scenes.

- From Chapter 6:

    The garden and its surroundings, then, were not, in themselves, outside the natural order of things; nor was Tom alarmed by his own unnatural abilities. Yet to some things his mind came back again and again, troubled: the constant fine weather, the rapid coming and going of the seasons and the times of day, the feeling of being watched.

    One night all his uneasiness came to a head. He had gone from his bed in the flat upstairs and crept down to the hall at about midnight, as usual; he had opened the garden door. He had found for the first time that it was night, too, in the garden. The moon was up, but clouds fled continuously across its face. Although there was this movement in the upper air, down below there was none: a great stillness lay within the garden, and a heavier heat than at any noon. Tom felt it: he unbuttoned his pyjama jacket and let it flap open as he walked.

One could smell the storm coming. Before Tom had reached the bottom of the garden, the moon had disappeared, obscured altogether by cloud. In its place came another light that seemed instantaneously to split the sky from top to bottom, and a few seconds later came the thunder.

Tom turned back to the house. As he reached the porch, the winds broke out into the lower air, with heavy rain and a deathly chilling of the temperature. Demons of the air seemed let loose in that garden; and, with the increasing frequency of the lightning. Tom could watch the foliage of the trees ferociously tossed and torn at by the wind, and, at the corner of the lawn, the tall, tapering fir-tree swinging to and fro, its ivy-wreathed arms struggling wildly in the tempest like the arms of a swaddling-child.

To Tom it seemed that the fir-tree swung more widely each time. 'It can't be blown over,' thought Tom. 'Strong trees are not often blown over.'

As if in answer to this, and while the winds still tore, there came the loudest thunder, with a flash of lightning that was not to one side nor even above, but seemed to come down into the garden itself, to the tree. The glare was blinding, and Tom's eyes closed against it, although only for a part of a second. When he opened them again, he saw the tree like one flame, and falling. In the long instant while it fell, there seemed to be a horrified silence of all winds; and, in that quiet, Tom heard something—a human cry—an 'Oh!' of the terror he himself felt. It came from above him—from the window of one of the upper rooms.

Then the fir-tree fell, stretching its length—although Tom did not know this until much later—along the grave-beds of the asparagus in the kitchen-garden. (Pearce, *Tom's Midnight Garden* 55-56)

- From Chapter 27:

    'I was married on Midsummer Day, a year or so after the great frost; Midsummer Eve was the eve of my wedding day. Doing the last of my packing that night, I remembered my skates, and that made me remember you, Tom. I'd kept my skates where I'd promised you that I would, and I knew that I had to leave them there, although it was so long since I'd seen you. I wrote a note of explanation and left it with the skates.'

    'I found it,' said Tom. 'Signed and dated.'

    'Dated Midsummer Eve, in one of the last years of the old century. That Midsummer Eve was very hot, sultry and thundery. I couldn't sleep. I thought of my wedding the next day, and, for the first time, I thought of all I would be leaving behind me: my childhood and all the times I had spent in the garden—in the garden with you, Tom.

    'There was a thunderstorm coming nearer, and there was lightning. I got out of bed and looked out of my window: I could see the meadow and the elm-tree and even the river-bank—I could see it all by the flashes of lightning.

    'Then I thought I would look at the garden, by the same light; I had a great longing to see it. I went into an empty bedroom at the back of the house, overlooking the garden, a spare bedroom.'

    'I think I know the one you mean,' said Tom. 'I stuck my head through the door, once.'

    'Well, I stood at the window and looked over the garden. The storm was very close; the lightning flashes made everything very clear. I could see the yew-trees and the fir-tree and the greenhouse, as if by daylight. Then I saw you.'

'Me?' cried Tom. 'But I don't understand. When? I didn't see you.'

'You never looked up. I think you had been walking round the garden, for you appeared from one of those little corner paths and walked across the lawn to the house porch. You looked as thin through as a piece of moonshine. You were wearing your pyjamas—they were pyjamas, weren't they, Tom? In those days, most boys wore nightshirts, and I didn't know of pyjamas. Your pyjama jacket was flapping open. I remember.

'You reached the porch, and I suppose you went indoors, for that was the last I saw of you. I stayed on at the window. I said to myself: "He's gone; but the garden is here. The garden will always be here. It will never change."

'Do you remember the tall fir-tree, Tom—with ivy all the way up? I've stood under it many a time, as a child, when there was a high wind, and felt the earth heaving under my feet, as if the roots were pulling like muscles. That Midsummer Eve, when the storm was at its worst, and I was watching it, a great wind caught the fir and—oh, Tom, it was terrible to see!—the lightning struck it, and it fell.'

There was a deep silence, and Tom remembered the silence he had heard after the falling of that tree, and the cry from the upper window that he had heard in it.

'And then I knew, Tom, that the garden was changing all the time, because nothing stands still, except in our memory.'

'And what happened next?' asked Tom.

'Oh, the next day, Abel complained of the fir-tree and that it had ruined one of his asparagus beds in its fall. . . . (211-12)

A New Theory About Time

This story has four boxes of time, one nesting inside another, as one of its frameworks.

- The small box: the garden in the past where Hatty and Tom meet (the world in Hatty's dream).

- The medium-sized box: the world in reality where Tom and Mrs. Bartholomew (Hatty) live.

- The large box: the world that involves all the times of the house, the grandfather clock and the angel.

- The extra-large box: the world where Pearce, the author of this story, and the readers live (It appears only once on p. 113).

Pearce, in the author's comment at the back of the book of the Iwanami Shoten edition, says that she did not write it as a fantasy, but it was an adaption of the new theory by J. W. Dunne, a British philosopher ("Mayonaka" 348). Dunne proposed that our experience of time as linear was an illusion brought about by human consciousness. He claims that in reality the past, the present and the future exist at the same time, and that when we dream, the illusion disappears and we can perceive the past and the future as we perceive the present ("Jon"). The reason *Tom's Midnight Garden* could be read as a fantasy might be that time and a dream play a significant role.

In Chapter 6, it has not been long since Tom visited the garden for the first time and he does not know Hatty yet. On the other hand, it is the last time Hatty sees Tom. It means that the beginning for Tom is the end for Hatty. Why does this inconsistency occur when Tom is assumed to have been in Hatty's dream and to have played together with her? I was confused when I had read through to the last chapter, recognizing that they are in the dream where the rule of the normal world does not work. However, I came to realize that there would be some reason why Pearce wrote the obviously inconsistent scene in the last chapter.

I would conclude that it is this inconsistency in time that the author intended to write.

The Revelation of St. John the Divine

"Hurry, hurry. . . . The hour is passing . . . passing" (Pearce, *Tom's Midnight Garden* 23). It is the house of Melbourne and the old grandfather clock that leads Tom into Hatty's dream. On that clock, the words, "Time No Longer," quoted from the Revelation of St. John the Divine at the end of the Bible are written, and the image of an angel is drawn. In the Book of Revelation, the phrases, which are said to be Christ's words, frequently appear: "I am the Alpha and the Omega" (*World English Bible*, Rev. 1.8); "I am the first and the last" (Rev. 1.17); "I am . . . the Beginning and the End" (Rev. 21.6).

Pearce might have shown the readers that this novel is apocalyptic literature by adopting the pattern that the first is the last from the Revelation.

The Revelation is at the end of the New Testament, and the Book of Genesis is at the beginning of the Old Testament. It is said that this order is significant. The Bible is written in concordance with the progress of time, from the creation of the universe to the doomsday, from the past through the present to the future. This is said to signify that God provided the beginning and the end at the same time. It means that the significance of history is comprehensible only when it is viewed from the end and that the end is the beginning of a new world. Pearce applied the order to the plot of this story in which Tom's beginning in the garden is Hatty's end of her life in the house, and the end of the association of Tom and Hatty in the garden is the beginning of the new stage of their lives.

A Dream Play

This story is a dream play where fairies appear. This is well expressed by the title, *Tom's Midnight Garden*. Hatty was married on Midsummer Day, on June 24. The previous day is the summer solstice. According to the old European religions and the folklores, that night young men and women went to the woods and devoted flower wreaths to the lovers or prayed for a happy marriage. It is said that fairies were rampant and the herbs were very effective that night. More details of these customs can be found in the bibliographical notes by Tsuneari Fukuda, the translator of *A Midsummer Night's Dream* by Shakespeare.

In one scene in *Tom's Midnight Garden*, the girl, Hatty, plays alone in the garden, and, seeking for an imaginary friend, she writes a letter to Oberon, the king of the fairies, and Tom finds it (77). Tom, who suddenly appears, is a fairy to Hatty.

Pearce, as a playwright and producer, produced educational programs for BBC, British Broadcasting Corporation (Takasugi 339). I imagine that she wrote *Tom's Midnight Garden* as if it were an open-air play performed in a courtyard in the afternoon in the seventeenth century.

II. A Comprehensible Story

Tom's Beginning Is Hatty's End.
I have mentioned that this story is modeled on the Book of Revelation, in the framework of a nest of times and that it is a dream play. Next, I will examine the coherence of the story concerning the description that Tom's beginning is Hatty's end.

The beginning and the end described here are not clear. Tom has entered the garden several times before Midsummer Eve, and Hatty (presumably ten years old) has watched him on the lawn in the garden through the yew trees, and, on another day, from the second floor of the house she has watched Tom, who was on the yew tree. Tom feels in the garden as if someone were watching him. I assume that Hatty, looking at Tom, thinks that an imaginary friend whom she created when she was younger has been embodied in Tom. In the author's comment at the back of the translation in the Iwanami edition, Pearce says that when Hatty grew old and began to live again her past in her memory, she could see Tom clearly ("Mayonaka" 350). It might mean that Mrs. Bartholomew lives in the new past when Tom existed from the beginning. It is an undeniable fact that Tom did not exist in Mrs. Bartholomew's past. The scene where Mrs. Bartholomew realizes that the garden is also changing, looking at the fir-tree which was struck by the lightning and fell on Midsummer Eve, might show the change into the new past. After that, she says, "nothing stands still, except in our memory" (212), but it is not true. Tom goes back to the house, tracing the path in the unknown garden which he has stepped into for the first time. On the other hand, Hatty instantaneously takes Tom into her memory of her childhood, and with that reset mind she sees Tom, her old friend, for the final time.

Tom's Resources and Hatty's Revelation
The incident that conveys most convincingly that the existence of Tom as an embodiment of her imaginary friend strongly encourages Hatty is the scene of the skating together on the river through Castleford to Ely in the lowland district. In order to get a pair of skates, Tom needs his resources. It is written in Chapter 21, Time and Time Again. One winter, Tom was asked to go skating together by Hatty, but he does not have skates. He works out a plan. He has her put her pair of skates in the secret place, underneath the floorboards of the bedroom cupboard. Because of this, Tom succeeds in making the angel in the grandfather clock step aside from the doorway to Tom, in other words, in dodging Time. By making use of the gap of Time, Tom succeeds in gaining Hatty's pair of skates in the real life, in the cupboards in his room in the Kitson's apartment. Tom's bedroom was once Hatty's. It is in the winter in 1895, some years after Hatty put her skates there, that Tom finds them. That winter the frost was over all England. It is written in the story that in the year there was a great frost recorded in history. The skating by the two occurred in the new past which Hatty had not experienced.

However, this small backflow of time was only a rebellion in a small time amid the large time. Although Tom decided to exchange his own time for the Eternity of Hatty's in the garden and play with Hatty for ever, the extra-large box of time, as if to make ends meet, lets Hatty run through her time at a high speed, and make her find a close relationship with young Barty (one of her cousins' friends), who is the first opposite sex that Hatty had a conversation with. That is the last evening for Tom to see Hatty, but Hatty sees him without his knowledge, and says farewell to him in her heart on Midsummer Eve about one year later.

Hatty, having met with a lover, is apt to forget about Tom after the evening of skating, but about one year later, while she is packing for the wedding, she remembers the skating and Tom. Thus, it is possible for Hatty, who knows everything, and for Tom, who does not know anything yet, to look at the same scene. This very scene is a revelation for Hatty.

Pearce and Her Grandmother

I will pick up, from the story, and try to assume details of the life of Hatty (= Mrs. Bartholomew).

She was born in presumably 1874, near the end of the Victorian era (1840s–1870s)[1], became an orphan due to her parents' death. She was raised at the Melbournes, her cousins' house. In 1896, at the age of twenty-two, she got married to Mr. Bartholomew, who was one of her cousin's friends, and lived in the lowland district. They had two boys, but they both were killed in World War I (1914–18). After that her husband bought the Melbournes's house, rebuilt it into an apartment house and rented it to tenants. After her husband's death, she moved to the third floor of this apartment house. She is now eighty-four years old. The year she got married is correct, but the other years are estimated from her age of marriage, twenty-two years old.

On the other hand, Tom Long is ten years old, which is considered to be the age when children begin to construct the concept of time. In the summer holidays, during which he had planned to play with his brother, he was sent to his aunt's to avoid infection of the measles from his brother. One day, during the stay being shut inside, he heard in the bed the clock strike thirteen, and being induced by the sound, he enters Mrs. Bartholomew's dream of retrospection.

The passageway between Hatty and Tom is a nursery room with the bed and the windows with bars on them. The room is also connected to Peter, his brother, who is in bed at home with measles. The name, "Peter," reminds me of *Peter Pan* by J. M. Barrie. I agree with the view of H. Carpenter that *Tom's Midnight Garden* is the reproduction of *Peter Pan* (*Secret* 219), for just as Wendy becomes an adult while Peter Pan remains an eternal boy, Hatty grows to be an adult instantaneously, leaving Tom behind although she lives on in the world of the past as a girl of the same age as Tom.

However, what is reassuring is that Tom recognizes the girl, Hatty, in the old woman's eyes. The author's comment referred to earlier says that the model of the old woman is Pearce's paternal grandmother (Pearce, "Mayonaka").

Echoes of this also appear in *The Way to Sattin Shore* (1983). In it, a wise old woman appears. She has two boys and is a grandmother on the father's side. It seems that Pearce was excessively interested in and had a deep affection for the grandmother.

A Comprehensible Story

The structure of *Tom's Midnight Garden* is adapted from apocalyptic literature in the Bible, and the framework consists of a dream-play in which traditional British fairies appear and a new idea about time by J. W. Dunne. And what Pearce aimed at in writing this story might be to present her old grandmother an old and new friend.

By reading this story in this way, *Tom's Midnight Garden* has been changed from an incomprehensible story into a comprehensible story.

Note

1. The Victorian era is from 1837 to 1901, but the age Mrs. Bartholomew refers to is its golden age, from the 1840s to the 1870s.

Works Consulted

Carpenter, Humphrey. *Secret Gardens: A Study of the Golden Age of Children's Literature*. 1985. London: Faber & Faber, 2009.

---. *Himitsu no Hanazono: Eibei Jido Bungaku no Ogon Jidai* [Secret Gardens: A Study of the Golden Age of Children's Literature] 秘密の花園：英米児童文学の黄金時代. Trans. Sadamatsu Tadashi 定松正. Tokyo: Kobian Shobo こびあん書房, 1988.

Fukuda, Tsuneari 福田恒存. "Kaidai" [Bibliographical Notes] 解題. Commentary. *Natsu no Yo no Yume; Arashi* [A Midsummer Night's Dream; The Tempest] 夏の夜の夢・あらし. By William Shakespeare. Trans. Fukuda. Tokyo: Shinchosha 新潮社, 1971. 112-20.

Gakken Henshubu 学研編集部, ed. *Kirisutokyo no Hon: Kyuseishu Iesu to Seisho no Nazo o Toku* [The Book of Christianity: Solving the Mystery of Christ the Savior and the Bible] キリスト教の本：救世主イエスと聖書の謎を解く. Vol. 1. Tokyo: Gakushu Kenkyusha 学習研究社, 1996. 2 vols.

Inokuma, Yoko 猪熊葉子, and Jingu Teruo 神宮輝夫. *Igirisu Jido Bungaku no Sakkatachi: Fantaji to Riarizumu* [The British Writers of Children's Literature—Fantasy and Realism] イギリス児童文学の作家たち：ファンタジーとリアリズム. Tokyo: Kenkyusha Shuppan 研究社出版, 1975.

"Jon Uiriamu Dan" [John William Dunne] ジョン・ウィリアム・ダン. *Wikipedia* ウィキペディア. 4 July 2016 <https://ja.wikipedia.org/wiki/ジョン・ウィリアム・ダン>.

Kiryu, Misao 桐生操. *Igirisu Fushigi na Yurei Yashiki* [Mysterious Haunted Houses in Britain] イギリス不思議な幽霊屋敷. Tokyo: PHP Kenkyujo PHP研究所, 1997.

Nihon Igirisu Jido Bungakukai [Japanese Society for Children's Literature in English] 日本イギリス児童文学会, ed. *Eibei Jido Bungaku Gaido: Sakuhin to Riron* [A Guide to British and American Literature for Children: The Works and the Theories] 英米児童文学ガイド：作品と理論. Tokyo: Kenkyusha Shuppan 研究社出版, 2001.

Pearce, Philippa. "Mayonaka no Niwa de no Koto" [About "The Midnight Garden"]

真夜中の庭でのこと. Pearce, *Tomu wa Mayonaka no Niwa de* 347-50. Rpt. from *Chosen for Children: An Account of the Books Which Have Been Awarded the Library Association Carnegie Medal, 1936–1965*. London: Library Association, 1967.

---. *Tom's Midnight Garden.* 1958. London: Puffin, 1976.

---. *Tomu wa Mayonaka no Niwa de* [Tom's Midnight Garden] トムは真夜中の庭で. Trans. Takasugi Ichiro 高杉一郎. 1975. Tokyo: Iwanami Shoten 岩波書店, 1998.

---. *The Way to Sattin Shore.* London: Kestrel, 1983.

Takasugi, Ichiro 高杉一郎. "Yakusha no Kotoba" [Translator's Word] 訳者のことば. Afterward. Pearce, *Tomu wa Mayonaka no Niwa de* 339-45.

Townsend, John Rowe. *Kodomo no Hon no Rekishi: Eigo Ken no Jido Bungaku* [Written for Children: An Outline of English-language Children's Literature] 子どもの本の歴史：英語圏の児童文学. Trans. Takasugi Ichiro 高杉一郎. Tokyo: Iwanami Shoten 岩波書店, 1982.

---. *Written for Children: An Outline of English-language Children's Literature.* London: Garnet Miller, 1965.

World English Bible. BibleGateway.com. 5 May 2016 <https://www.biblegateway.com>.

Chapter XIII

The Negative Aspects in Human Nature
—Comparing the Two Editions of Japanese Translation of *The Hundred Dresses* by Eleanor Estes—

> **"I got a hundred dresses home."**
> —Eleanor Estes, *The Hundred Dresses*

Eleanor Estes
The Hundred Dresses
Illustrated by Louis Slobodkin

New York: Harcourt, 1944

* Japanese edition: Estes, Eleanor. *Hyakumai no Kimono*. Trans. Momoko Ishii. Tokyo: Iwanami Shoten, 1954.

* Revised edition: Estes, Eleanor. *Hyakumai no Doresu*. Trans. Momoko Ishii. Tokyo: Iwanami Shoten, 2006.

This is a short novel written in America in 1944. It was reprinted in 1972. In 1954, the Japanese translation by Momoko Ishii was published. Fifty two years later, it was revised by the same translator with a different title. The reason for its long standing might be that it deals with the theme, old and new, "bullying," which is deeply related to human nature. Bullying exists anywhere and anytime. Japan is no exception. In particular, bullying in schools continues to be a problem and abroad this aspect of Japanese life draws attention. However, when I read the new edition of the Japanese translation, I found that the publishers needed to revise it.

Some illustrations, the table of contents and the postscript by the translator are added in the new edition. The translator says that Eleanor Estes's own experience in her elementary school is reflected on this story. In her class during World War I, there was a Polish girl who wore the same clothes every day and moved to another school in the middle of the term (Ishii, Afterword 90).

The story is about the three girls, Peggy, the bully, Wanda, her victim and Madeline, who is in-between. The story takes place over two months of a school term. In reading the two editions, I was motivated to change my reading concerning the three phrases: one is about a difference of nuance and the other two are about the correction of the mistranslations.

#1
The original:
> . . . and Boggins Heights was <u>no place to live</u>. (Estes 9, emphasis mine)

In the old Japanese edition:
> Boggins Heights is an <u>intolerable</u> place to live in. (Ishii, *Hyakumai no Kimono* 9, emphasis mine)

In the new Japanese edition:
> Boggins Heights is <u>not a place for humans to live in</u>. (Ishii, *Hyakumai no Doresu* 15, emphasis mine)

#2
The original:
> <u>Maddie remembered her telling</u> about one of her dresses, a pale

blue one with cerise-colored trimmings. And she remembered another that was brilliant jungle green with a red sash. "You'd look like a Christmas tree in that," the girls had said in pretended admiration. (Estes 36-38, emphasis mine)

In the old Japanese edition:

Maddie said <u>to Wanda</u>. . . . <u>Wanda</u> said. . . . (Ishii, *Hyakumai no Kimono* 35, emphasis mine)

In the new Japanese edition:

Madeline remembered <u>Wanda telling her [Madeline] about</u> a pale blue one with cerise-colored trimmings. . . . <u>the other girls in the class</u> said. . . . (Ishii, *Hyakumai no Doresu* 40-42, emphasis mine)

#3

The original:

"And boy! This shows she really liked us. It shows she got our letter and this is her way of saying that everything's all right. And <u>that's that</u>," she said with finality. (Estes 76, emphasis mine)

In the old Japanese edition:

". . . <u>I am relieved, to begin with</u>," Peggy said with finality. (Ishii, *Hyakumai no Kimono* 69, emphasis mine)

In the new Japanese edition:

". . . <u>Everything has been done</u>," Peggy said with finality. (Ishii, *Hyakumai no Doresu* 77, emphasis mine)

The change in #1 is about the negative evaluation of Boggins Heights, where Wanda lives. Prejudice and discrimination against the poverty and the poor area in the countryside in America around 1916 (estimated from the author's age, ten) can be observed. Wanda's family were immigrants from Poland and were very poor.

In the translation of #2, the subject and the object are switched. In the old edition, Maddie talks to Wanda about Wanda's dress. On the other hand, in the new edition, Wanda talks to Maddie about Wanda's dress. It is clear that this is the correction of the expression in the old edition, and errors like this may have been behind the decision to publish a new edition, for this part is directly connected to the main theme of this story. At the end of the story Madeline finds that she and Peggy were the models of the design pictures Wanda had sent to them.

I was confused with the part mentioned as #2 in the old edition, but that in the new edition made clearer the author's intention that these two pictures are drawn for Peggy and Madeline, and it made me have a higher regard for this novel. By the way, this part of the edition translated by Tomoko Nakayama is the same as the old edition translated by Ishii.

The translations in the old and new editions of #3 show the difference of Peggy's impression of Wanda. The Japanese expression, "mazu" [to begin with], conveys an impression that makes the reader expect the improvement in relationship between Peggy and Wanda. On the other hand, in the new edition, "Nanimokamo sunda" [Everything has been done.] does not make the readers expect the further relationship with Wanda. I believe that the Japanese translation in the new edition might be correct on the grounds that Madeline thinks she will never see Wanda and regrets that she could not persuade Peggy to stop bullying Wanda because she was given Peggy's old dress.

Every time I read this book, various thoughts are provoked in me. At first, I was impressed by what seemed to be Peggy's innovative and rational ideas. Peggy thinks that Wanda could create the fantastic designs and won the first prize in the contest owing to Peggy's teasing and making fun of Wanda by asking how many dresses Wanda has. At first, this rationale was persuasive to me as it was to Madeline. However, later, I thought that the idea was self-centered and cunning, and Madeline's plain and ordinary interpretation that she had reached after having thought it over was correct.

Adding to that, when I read the new edition, I thought what Peggy did was nothing but bullying. What is clearer from the revised translation is that Peggy was a power holder who felt pleasure in bullying the weak. What Wanda did was the expression of her resistance to Peggy, but Peggy could not understand it. Peggy meant to make Wanda stop telling a lie. The other girls cannot accept Wanda's assertion that the hundred pictures of dresses kept in her home are the hundred dresses. Although her talent might cut open the path to the future, before that, Wanda needs to gain the language that makes her understood, and it should be accomplished first in the relationship with her friends. Writing the reply to the letter from Peggy and Madeline was the first step for Wanda, who could hardly read English books.

Lonely Wanda might have wanted friends, and on a beautiful day in October, she at last found the interest she could share with her classmates, which is a dress. She talked to Peggy, who was the most popular and beautiful girl in her class. The saving grace of this story is that although Wanda is in the position of the weak, she loves what is beautiful more than anything else.

Although the author has Madeline say that Peggy is a good girl, I do not agree. The person who bullies others is said to be very sensitive to who is stronger. Once Peggy finds that Wanda is much better in drawing than herself, she accommodates herself to Wanda. Whereas Madeline is moved by Wanda's kindness in drawing Madeline's figure in the pictures, Peggy declares, based on her self-seeking ideas, that Wanda loves them, and Peggy will not accept her own fault, nor try to revive the relationship with Wanda.

This is a rare book to me which conveys softly the negative aspects of human nature: the display of own power, accommodation to the power and self-centeredness with which one tries to cancel out what is unfavorable to oneself.

Works Consulted

Estes, Eleanor. *The Hundred Dresses*. 1944. Orlando, Fla.: Harcourt, 1972.

Ishii, Momoko 石井桃子. Afterword. *Hyakumai no Doresu* [The Hundred Dresses] 百まいのドレス. By Eleanor Estes. Trans. Ishii. Tokyo: Iwanami Shoten 岩波書店, 2006. 87-92.

---, trans. *Hyakumai no Doresu* [The Hundred Dresses] 百まいのドレス. By Eleanor Estes. Trans. Ishii. Tokyo: Iwanami Shoten 岩波書店, 2006.

---, trans. *Hyakumai no Kimono* [The Hundred Dresses] 百まいのきもの. By Eleanor Estes. Tokyo: Iwanami Shoten 岩波書店, 1954.

Nakayama, Tomoko 中山知子, trans. "Hyakumai no Doresu" [The Hundred Dresses] 百まいのドレス. By Eleanor Estes. *Shonen Shojo Sekai Bungaku Zenshu* [The Collection of World Children's Literature] 少年少女世界文学全集. Eds. Namekawa Michio 滑川道夫, et al. Trans. Yazaki Genkuro 矢崎源九郎, et al. Vol. 15. Tokyo: Gakushu Kenkyusha 学習研究社, 1969. 307-39.

Chapter XIV

The Man Who Wanted to Become a King
—*The Little Prince* and *The Wisdom of the Sands* as Its Parent Body—

Antoine de Saint-Exupéry
Le Petit Prince [The Little Prince]

New York: Reynal and Hitchcock, 1943

* Japanese edition: Saint-Exupéry, Antoine. *Hoshi no Ojisama*. Trans. Aro Naito. Tokyo: Iwanami Shoten, 1953.

Le Petit Prince [The Little Prince] by Saint-Exupéry (1900–44) was published in 1943. Seventy years has passed since then, but it has kept its popularity and continues to attract new readers. In Christmas season every year, new translations and versions with beautiful covers are displayed on the shelves of bookstores, serving as suitable items for presents. It is like the Bible for some people.

I have not admired the prince's selfishness for a long time, but I dared to read the story again and was amazed that it was full of mystery. I decided to investigate further into what the author intended to convey in this book.

I mainly used Japanese translations for reference: one is *Saint-Exupéry: A Biography* (1994) by Stacy Schiff, who was the editor of a major American publisher, and the other is *Antoine de Saint-Exupéry: The Life and Death of*

The Little Prince (1993) by Paul Webster, an British newspaper reporter resident in Paris. For this chapter I drew on Schiff and Webster for their insights into this writer.

First, I will outline Saint-Exupéry's life.

I. Saint-Exupéry

Writing Poems and Enthusiasm for Flight
Antoine de Saint-Exupéry, was born in 1900 as the first son of a noble family in Lyon, France. His father, a count, died when Saint-Exupéry was four years old. He spent his childhood at the mansions of his maternal grandmother and grand-aunt. That is to say, he was a real prince. He was sensitive and wrote poems, and read them to his four siblings and his mother. He is said to be very tyrannical and hit his younger brother for not listening to him quietly. According to the recollection by one of his classmates and his academic record at his alma mater, when he was around fifteen, he was a "dreamer" and not good at school, but good at writing epics and drawing sketches (Schiff, *Saint-Exupéry* 31-35, 54; Estang 17-18).

In 1909, six years after the Wright brothers succeeded in the first flight, Louis Charles-Joseph Blériot flew across the English Channel. The zeal for aircrafts was enhanced in France. French youngsters longed for the sky. Saint-Exupéry was one of them, and he was such a science boy that he designed the motor of a flying bicycle (Webster 64-67).

When he was nineteen years old, he took the examination for the naval academy, which was the elite track, but failed twice. Unwillingly, he entered an art school. After that, he underwent military service and entered the flying corps. He gained a civil pilot's license at the age of twenty-one, and a military pilot's license at the age of twenty-two (Schiff, *Saint-Exupéry* 72-74, 79, 82-94). According to Webster, his best friend, Léon Werth, says that Saint-Exupéry was an excessive worrier and his mood changed easily, and that he could not be in a happy mood for a long time (242). For the sake of his fiancé, he worked as a bookkeeper, or as a salesman, which were safe jobs, but it did not work well, and the engagement was broken off. After that, he worked for a civil airline thanks to connections to his teacher at his school. Although he was not very skillful at piloting, he knew that he needed to fly to give him mental stability and a fresh outlook on life (Schiff, *Saint-Exupéry* 95-118; Webster 98-114, 152-53, 215).

He Wrote on the Consistent Theme

Saint-Exupéry's first work is *Courrier Sud* [Southern Mail] published in 1929. This book was written when he entered Lacoste Yale, a civil airline which was a pioneer of regular post service. He worked for two years as a manager of the airport at Cape Juby, a relay base in the Sahara, and wrote the book in solitary and severe circumstances (Schiff, *Saint-Exupéry* 3-17, 127-58). After that, Saint-Exupéry wrote *Vol de nuit* [Night Flight], *Terre des hommes* [Wind, Sand and Stars], *Pilote de guerre* [Flight to Arras], *The Little Prince* and lastly *Citadelle* [The Wisdom of the Sands], which is an incomplete epic. According to the biography by Schiff, all of these works are written on the same theme, that is, "the need to barter oneself for a greater good." He also had continuous interest in "how to reconcile an individual's thirst for profit with some social good" and "how to nourish and motivate man in a machine age" (Schiff, *Saint-Exupéry* 289, 444).

The Influence by the Philosophers

Nietzsche is a German philosopher who died in 1900, when Saint-Exupéry was born. From the 1890s, Nietzsche's works had been widely read. It is said that he influenced the works of André Gide. Saint-Exupéry contributed to La Nouvelle Revue Française (NRF), the magazine which Gide first published in 1908 (Schiff, *Saint-Exupéry* 176; Webster 110; Watanabe and Nishio 593, 707-08). French people love debate and France has given the world the greatest number of philosophers. Saint-Exupéry also had many books of thought at hand, especially by Pascal, Nietzsche and Dostoyevsky. What is common to these three thinkers is the pursuit of Jesus Christ. Pascal (1623–62), a

French religious philosopher, in *Pensées*, the fragmentary thoughts, tried to approach Jesus not rationally but emotionally. Nietzsche (1844–1900), in *Also sprach Zarathustra* [Thus Spoke Zarathustra] (1883–85), advocated the conversion of all the old values and declared his stand as the anti-Christ. It is known that Saint-Exupéry read this book in 1926. Dostoyevsky, a Russian man of letters (1821–81), wrote in his novel, *Crime and Punishment* (1866), about an arrogant young man, who commits a murder, and later returns to Jesus Christ. Saint-Exupéry said he had felt that he had touched something magnificent when he read this book. They recognized in Jesus's way of life what a human being is and how a human being should live, and expressed them in their own words (Schiff, *Saint-Exupéry* 58; Webster 139, 244-45; Saito 67-68; Estang 216, 233).

Webster says Saint-Exupéry revered the power of Pascal's words as if they came from God (244-45).

The New Words and *The Wisdom of the Sands*

The reason Saint-Exupéry awoke to politics was that he had witnessed the war with his own eyes when he visited Spain, being sent there by the newspaper to report the civil war (Schiff, *Saint-Exupéry* 272, 281-82). Saint-Exupéry saw the people suffer from the severe circumstances without a good leader. He began to consider unifying public feelings with a power of words and leading the people to a right direction as his mission.

In that year, he started to write *The Wisdom of the Sands*. The protagonist is a young king of the Berbers in northern Africa, who has succeeded his father king. He endeavors to create powerful words which will uplift his people and lead them into action. The style of the story is solemn as is in the Bible, or with an air of the medieval period. The Berber people are the natives (The Moors) whom Saint-Exupéry encountered at Cap Juby when he was sent to rescue a mail plane. They were enemies at one time, and friends at another. Saint-Exupéry won their hearts and was trusted by them. He was given an honorable name, "Captain of the Birds" by the head of the tribe. This is the basic idea of *The Wisdom of the Sands*. He went across to America holding lovingly the manuscripts of fifteen chapters out of two hundred and nineteen chapters of the book. *The Wisdom of the Sands* has more than nine hundred pages, to which he dedicated himself heart and soul. He continued to write it until the last minute of his life, along with *Flight to Arras* and *The Little Prince* (Schiff, *Saint-Exupéry* 5-30; "Kankosha" 6-7). Saint-Exupéry regarded *The Wisdom of the Sands* as his most important work, and he thought that the other works were only studies for it (qtd. in Yamazaki 287-88).

In *The Wisdom of the Sands*, the young king frequently calls his late father or invisible gods and prays to them, asking for their help. He is a solitary leader who is on the top of the high mountain, looking down over his land for the inspiration in order that he can lead his people.

In 1940, as demoralized France was being defeated by Germany, Saint-Exupéry saw from his plane the culture and the civilization of his country collapsing in an instance. At this moment, he strongly felt again necessity of a good leader (Webster 292-94). The king in *The Wisdom of the Sands*, who suffers from the conflict with the king of the neighboring country and grieves over the Berbers' idleness and the useless arguments, is exactly Saint-Exupéry himself. In *Flight to Arras*, he writes about the hero who, after France was defeated by Germany, goes across to America and, being troubled by the idleness and gossipy argument of exiled French people, he advocates Christian civilization and humanism and tries to urge America to participate in World War II.

Saint-Exupéry says that he could not perform his "alchemy" in writing *Flight to Arras* as he worked in haste and did not have enough time to polish the plan (Schiff, *Saint-Exupéry* 398).

The Exchange of Presents

Among the factors common to these three works, there is a logic that building up a community by collaboration is the exchange of each power.

In Chapter 24 in *Flight to Arras*, Saint-Exupéry says that France joined the Allies in the early stage of World War II and sent a relief corps to the countries of north Europe, that this operation had a background of Christmas/Christian spirit, and that he demands this spirit from America, that is, to offer their lives, the ultimate present.

In *The Little Prince*, the prince and the pilot walk in the desert and find a well and drink the water of life. The pilot gives the prince water, and the prince presents the pilot a laughing star in return.

In *The Wisdom of the Sands*, the Berbers, led by the young king, make the fortress city secure by the efforts of sentries, craftsmen, dancers, and a geometrician. In Europe a fortress represents a small form of civilization, a tribe or a city.

The Little Prince, Flight to Arras and *The Wisdom of the Sands*
While Saint-Exupéry wrote *The Wisdom of the Sands*, he often read it aloud to his friends, but they did not rate it highly. The person who placed the highest value on it was Hélène de Vogüé, who was recognized as his patron from his twenties. She was a businesswoman who loved literature and was a safe haven for Saint-Exupéry. It is said that when she said to him, "You are a little like Christ when you write your *Citadelle* [The Wisdom of the Sands]," he nodded quietly (Schiff, *Saint-Exupéry* 414-15; Webster 228-29).

I am amazed at how high his ideal for human beings is and, particularly, that he was concerned about mankind like Jesus Christ. He was not a very pious Christian. He seems to have had an image of God as the source of "a greater good" (Schiff, *Saint-Exupéry* 59-60).

In the first volume of *The Wisdom of the Sands*, the young king considers the woman who tells a lie because of her anxiety. This beautiful woman cannot express herself honestly, and continues to resist. He does not abandon her and endeavors to correct her, which he regards as his trial given to him by God.

This woman is compared to the rose with thorns in *The Little Prince*, and his wife, Consuelo, is said to be a model. In both of the stories, the protagonists take responsibilities for the women whom they have chosen and discharge their obligations, devoting their love as a medieval knight.

In the second volume, the father king's best friend, "a true geometrician," who is a wise man who resembles Pascal, appears. He is compared to the fox in *The Little Prince*. The fox's advice makes the prince realize that the rose is a treasure for him. He also learns from the fox how to make friends and how lively a day could become by "observing the proper rites" (Woods 82).

This wise man in the desert reminds me of the people whom Saint-Exupéry empathized with and respected. I am reminded of Nietzsche's "love of fate"—the idea that the love you feel now is inevitable and there is no other possibility—concerning love, and the words by Sylvia Hamilton, a journalist, who was Saint-Exupéry's girlfriend in New York, concerning how to make friends and about "the rites." The greater part of *The Little Prince* was written in her living room. This American woman approached Saint-Exupéry in 1942 before he wrote *The Little Prince*, having been moved by his *Wind, Sand and Stars*. One day, when Saint-Exupéry didn't appear at her residence at the appointed time, she said, "My heart begins to dance when I know you are coming" (Schiff, *Saint-Exupéry* 138, 239, 372-79; Saito 67-68; Estang 43-44, 136-39, 150). In the story, the fox says, "If, for example, you came at four o'clock in the afternoon, then at three o'clock I shall begin to be happy" (Woods 81). The fox meant that he wanted to decide the time to meet.

However, the prince learns that although the fox is one of his friends, he will go away, only leaving the memories behind, and that what the prince wants are a little sheep which will protect the rose and a human friend who will draw a picture of it. Having learned these from the fox, the prince goes over to the pilot to make friends.

In *The Little Prince*, the prince asks the pilot to draw a sheep for him, and the pilot says, "If anybody wants a sheep, that is a proof that he exists" (Woods 21). Six years after their encounter and the departure, the pilot tries to prove the prince's identity. What was the significance of the encounter with the prince to the pilot?

In the story, when the two begin to walk searching for water, the prince says, "Water may also be good for the heart" (Woods 88). The prince is the pilot's mind temporarily separated from him. After a while, the pilot, holding the prince in his arms, discovers a well in the dawn. The water drawn from the well by the pilot pleases the prince. This scene is very beautiful. It is the moment when the mind and the body are bound together firmly. It is the scene where the community is made up by their collaboration.

As I mentioned before, although *Flight to Arras* accomplished the mission to urge America to participate in the war, its structure is said to be imbalanced. As far as the chapter 24, it is for the most part the record of his own experience of his reconnaissance flights, from the chapter 25 to 28 is a philosophical inquiry into Christian civilization and the human virtues, which is similar to the world of *The Wisdom of the Sands*. Saint-Exupéry's main interest is in the coexistence of the happiness of individuals and the public interest. His flight to Arras in 1940 seems to have awakened his love for his mother country, France.

In short, in wartime, individuals who have lived separately like selfish children are united with a strong tie by joining the services and becoming soldiers and begin to pursue the public interest of protecting their fatherland.

Half a year after he wrote *Flight to Arras*, he began to write *The Little Prince* (Schiff, *Saint-Exupéry* 378). The prince, who is a selfish individual, decides to sacrifice himself overcoming the fear in order to protect France and the rose, and put it into practice. Thus, it can be said that these two works are based on *The Wisdom of the Sands*.

In his real life, while he continued to write in America, he worked upon the military, using every connection, to fly again. And, at last, he got permission to rejoin "the 2/33" squadron. It was tempting fate for a 44 years old man to participate in the war (Schiff, *Saint-Exupéry* 395-403). Saint-Exupéry said that *The Wisdom of the Sands* was his "posthumous work" (Schiff, *Saint-Exupéry* 337). *The Little Prince* is the story about a selfish child who wants to be a soldier. The destination that the prince heads for, parting from his beloved rose and friends, seems to be the battle field and God's realm.

II. The Little Prince and "The Hymn of the Pearl"

Reading the materials led me to think that the relationship between the prince and the pilot can be compared to that between Jesus Christ and one of his twelve apostles, a martyr, Judas Thomas. According to an apocrypha, in the middle of the first century he was ordered by Jesus to go to India to propagate and achieved magnificent results. However, in the end, he incurred the anger of the king in that region, and was captured and executed (Arai 191-282). His death might be compared to Jesus's death. Judas is thought to have written "The Hymn of the Pearl," the dedication to the life of Jesus Christ, which includes Indian and Iranian folklores. This story has the same pattern as *The Little Prince* and the theme is self-recognition. The outline is as follows.

* * *

The prince in the kingdom in the East is sent to Egypt, parting from the family in the homeland to fetch a pearl guarded by a snake. It was a rite of passage for him to become a king. In Egypt, he falls into a sleep and forgets his mission and what he is supposed to be, and becomes like a slave. However, "the calling" from the letter of his father and mother awakened the recognition of his mission, and succeeds in gaining the pearl. He returns home, guided by the letter, and puts on the glistening garment which he took off at his departure (Arai 265-74).

* * *

I will compare this with *The Little Prince*:
    Saint-Exupéry had an innate sense of mission that he must express his thinking. He recognized himself as a prince sent to this world by God to accomplish his mission. He embodied it in his work, *The Wisdom of the Sands*. However, it was not completed. Instead, *The Little Prince*, in which the essence of a part of *The Wisdom of the Sands* is expressed, accomplished

its mission more effectively than the author himself expected.

In 1935, while he was breaking the record for a flight between Paris and Saigon, he met with a forced-landing on the Libya Desert and was rescued by the nomads. This experience seems to be in the background of the story (Schiff, *Saint-Exupéry* 258-63). The letter in "The Hymn of the Pearl" can be compared to the voice of the little prince, who asks the pilot to "draw him a sheep," which awakened Saint-Exupéry to his own mission, and the pearl which the prince fetches back is the sheep that Saint-Exupéry draws and is *The Wisdom of the Sands*, the story of human beings.

III. Conclusion

Saint-Exupéry was born to an aristocratic family and had knights in his ancestry (Schiff, *Saint-Exupéry* 31-32). The family upheld the ideals of kingship (the leader of the people). He was gifted with the talent to write poems. He was sensitive to the effects created by the arrangement of words, by which plain words can be made luscious, and he had a sense of mission that he must express himself. He believed he must use "the new magical words" that he had created and that the words must absorb all contradictions. He had discovered it in Pascal and Nietzsche and challenged them in writing *The Wisdom of the Sands*.

What is common to these three is that they have wide perspectives. Pascal, who is known for Pascal's principle, was a geometrician, physician, inventor, and religious philosopher. *Pensées* is a philosophical thinking on the greatness and the pettiness of human beings. Nietzsche's philosophy has had great influence on generations of people. His work, *Zarathustra*, is a story of a person who achieves enlightenment on the mountain and, coming down to the field, imparts wisdom to the people. The style is similar to *The Wisdom of the Sands*. Saint-Exupéry, as a pioneer pilot, literally gained a higher and wider perspective than the former men of letters, and this generated his unique considerations about human beings.

Saint-Exupéry resembles Pascal in having multiple talents. He loved mathematics, physics and invention. He often applied for patents for his mysterious inventions. In his notes taken since 1930, he made memos about politics and economy, which were totally different from literature. He also was versed in contemporary studies such as Freud's psychology and Einstein's theory of relativity (Schiff, *Saint-Exupéry* 229, 289-90).

All these learnings were poured into *The Wisdom of the Sands*, and the young king meditates on the economy, patriotism and the politics of his land. Because of that, this novel is conceptual and difficult to understand.

The reason *The Little Prince* is relatively easy to understand is that it is a love story with an explicit plot. I regard "the sheep in the box" which the prince asks the pilot to draw as the unfinished *The Wisdom of the Sands* because Saint-Exupéry could not foresee whether either *The Wisdom of the Sands* or *The Little Prince* would be successful or not. The prince's fear that the sheep might eat the rose would connote Saint-Exupéry's anxiety for the predicaments which might fall on his wife, Consuelo, who can be compared to the rose, and his fear that he might not protect his wife as a husband, as a result of the failure of these two works, and also would imply his fear for the fall of France. "The sheep with a muzzle without the lead" can be read as Saint-Exupéry's regret to *The Wisdom of the Sands*, which he did not have time to revise or amend because he had to go to the front, or as disastrous France without a powerful leader. "The fight between the sheep and the flower" might suggest the difference in the way of living and the desire between men and women, or the relationship between a soldier (a war) and a woman (civilization).

The key with which the riddle of *The Little Prince* can be solved was in *The Wisdom of the Sands*. I was often amazed at the range of Saint-Exupéry's interests. Luc Estang, a poet and the author of *Saint-Exupéry* describes *The Wisdom of the Sands* as "a bazaar of Oriental ideas" (194).

After the expiration of the translation right of *The Little Prince* in 2005, new translations have been repeatedly published. In June of 2011, Keijiro Suga published a Japanese translation, *Hoshi no Ojisama* [The Little Prince].

The originality of this translation is symbolized in the words for I and you. He uses, instead of "boku" and "kimi," "ore" and "omae," which in Japanese language are used by males in less formal situations. Suga turned the noble boy into a street-kid-like boy without kith or kin. *The Little Prince*, which has begun to allow such new interpretations, has taken on increasingly an aspect of the Bible for some people of today. In the center, the Jesus Christ figure stands as an image of an ideal man for some readers in Western countries.

In the story, the prince grieves over his failings and says that he will not be a good king. Masaru Sato, in his *Hajimete no Shukyoron* [Studies on Religion for Beginners], says that Christ means a person on whom oil is poured, that is, a king who has an authority to save people (176-77). I believe that Saint-Exupéry, while he wrote *The Wisdom of the Sands* and *The Little Prince*, tried to become a new king through contemplation about the things of the world and to save mankind.

Works Consulted

Akiyama, Satoko 秋山さと子. *Satori no Bunseki: Bukkyo to Yungu Shinrigaku to no Setten* [An Analysis of Enlightenment: Where Buddhism and Jungian Psychology Meet] 悟りの分析：仏教とユング心理学との接点. 1980. Tokyo: PHP Kenkyujo PHP研究所, 1991.

Arai, Sasagu 荒井献, trans. "Shito Yuda Tomasu no Gyoden" [Acts of Thomas] 使徒ユダ・トマスの行伝. *Shin'yaku Seisho Gaiten* [The New Testament Apocrypha] 新約聖書外典. Trans. Arai, et al. Seisho no Sekai [The World of the Bible] 聖書の世界. Supplementary vol. 3. Tokyo: Kodansha 講談社, 1974. 191-282.

---. *Tomasu ni Yoru Fukuinsho* [The Gospel of Thomas] トマスによる福音書. Tokyo: Kodansha 講談社, 1994.

Estang, Luc. *San-Tegujuperi no Sekai: Hoshi to Sabaku no Hazama ni* サン=テグジュペリの世界：星と砂漠のはざまに. Trans. Yamazaki Yoichiro 山崎庸一郎. Tokyo: Iwanami Shoten 岩波書店, 1990. Trans. of *Saint-Exupéry*. Paris:

Editions du Seuil, 1956.

Hashizume, Daisaburo 橋爪大三郎, and Osawa Masachi 大澤真幸. *Fushigi na Kirisutokyo* [Wonders In Christianity] ふしぎなキリスト教. Tokyo: Kodansha 講談社, 2011.

Jonas, Hans. *Gunoshisu no Shukyo: Iho no Kami no Fukuin to Kirisutokyo no Tansho* グノーシスの宗教：異邦の神の福音とキリスト教の端緒. Trans. Akiyama Satoko 秋山さと子, and Irie Ryohei 入江良平. Kyoto: Jinbun Shoin 人文書院, 1986. Trans. of *The Gnostic Religion: The Message of the Alien God & the Beginnings of Christianity*. Boston: Beacon Press, 1958.

"Kankosha Tachi no Oboegaki" [Notes by the Publishers] 刊行者たちの覚え書. Foreword. Saint-Exupéry, *Josai* 3-12.

Nietzsche, Friedrich Wilhelm. *Tsaratusutora ha Ko Itta* [Also sprach Zarathustra] ツァラトゥストラはこう言った. Trans. Higami Hidehiro 氷上英広. Tokyo: Iwanami Shoten 岩波書店, 1967. Trans. of *Also Sprach Zarathustra* [Thus Spoke Zarathustra]. Chemnitz: Schmeitzner. 1883-85.

Nihon Seishogaku Kenkyujo [Japanese Biblical Institute] 日本聖書学研究所, ed. *Shin'yaku Seisho Gaiten II* [The New Testament Apocrypha II] 新約聖書外典 II. Seisho Gaiten Giten [The Apocrypha and Pseudepigrapha] 聖書外典偽典. Vol. 7. Tokyo: Kyobunkan 教文館, 1976.

Pascal, Blaise. *Panse: Meisoroku* パンセ：冥想録. Trans. Tsuda Yutaka 津田穣. Tokyo: Shinchosha 新潮社, 1952. Trans. of *Pensées*. 1670.

Saint-Exupéry, Antoine. *Citadelle* [The Wisdom of the Sands]. Paris: Gallimard, 1948.

---. *Courrier Sud* [Southern Mail]. Paris: Gallimard, 1929.

---. *Hoshi no Ojisama* [The Little Prince] 星の王子さま. Trans. Naito Aro 内藤濯. Tokyo: Iwanami Shoten 岩波書店, 1953.

---. *Josai* [The Wisdom of the Sands] 城砦 I. Trans. Yamazaki Yoichiro 山崎庸一郎, and Awazu Norio 粟津則雄. 1962. Tokyo: Misuzu Shobo みすず書房, 1976.

---. *Le Petit Prince* [The Little Prince]. New York: Reynal and Hitchcock, 1943.

---. *Pilote de guerre* [Flight to Arras]. New York: Harcourt, 1942.

---. *Terre des hommes* [Wind, Sand and Stars]. Paris: Gallimard, 1939.

---. *Vol de nuit* [Night Flight]. Paris: Gallimard, 1931.

Saito, Takashi 齋藤孝. *San Tegujuperi: Taisetsh na Koto o Wasurenai Shonen Ryoku* [Saint-Exupéry: "Juvenile's Potential" not to Forget What is Essential] サン=テグジュペリ：大切なことを忘れない「少年力」. Tokyo: Daiwa Shobo 大和書房, 2006.

Sato, Masaru 佐藤優. *Hajimete no Shukyoron: Mienai Sekai no Gyakushu* [Studies on Religion for Beginners: a Counterattack by the Invisible World] はじめての宗教論：見えない世界の逆襲　右巻. Tokyo: Nihon Hoso Shuppan Kyokai 日本放送出版協会, 2009.

Schiff, Stacy. *Saint-Exupéry: A Biography.* New York: Henry Holt, 1994. London: Chatto & Windus, 1994.

---. *San-Tegujuperi no Shogai* [Saint-Exupéry: A Biography] サン=テグジュペリの生涯. Trans. Higaki Tsugiko 桧垣嗣子. Tokyo: Shinchosha 新潮社, 1997.

Sfar, Joann, and Brigitte Findakly, adapt. *Hoshi no Ojisama: Bando Deshineban* 星の王子さま：バンド・デシネ版. By Antoine de Saint-Exupéry. Trans. Ikezawa Natsuki 池澤夏樹. Tokyo: Sankuchuari Shuppan サンクチュアリ出版, 2011. Trans. of *Le Petit Prince: D'après L'oeuvre D'Antoine De Saint-Exupéry* [The Little Prince]. Paris: Gallimard, 2008.

Suga, Keijiro 管啓次郎, trans. *Hoshi no Ojisama* [The Little Prince] 星の王子さま. By Antoine de Saint-Exupéry. Tokyo: Kadokawa Shoten 角川書店, 2011.

Watanabe, Jiro 渡邊二郎, and Nishio Kanji 西尾幹二, eds. *Niche o Shiru Jiten: Sono Shin'en to Tamenteki Sekai* [A Dictionary on Nietzsche: His Depths and the Multifaceted World] ニーチェを知る事典：その深淵と多面的世界. Tokyo: Chikuma Shobo 筑摩書房, 2013.

Webster, Paul. *Hoshi no Ojisama o Sagashite* 星の王子さまを探して. Trans. Nagashima Ryozo 長島良三. Tokyo: Kadokawa Shoten 角川書店, 1996. Trans. of *Saint-Exupéry: Vie et Mort du Petit Prince* [Antoine de Saint-Exupéry: The Life and Death of The Little Prince]. Paris: Éd. du Félin, 1993.

Woods, Katherine, trans. *The Little Prince.* By Antoine de Saint-Exupéry. Ed. Fukuda Rikutaro 福田陸太郎. Tokyo: Eikosha 英光社, 1966.

Yamazaki, Yoichiro 山崎庸一郎. Commentary. Saint-Exupéry, *Josai* 285-300.

Yume Project 夢プロジェクト, ed. *Joshiki to shite Shitteokitai Sekai no Tetsugakusha 50nin: Karera wa Nani o Kangae Watakushitachi ni Nani o Nokoshitanoka*

[Fifty Philosophers over the World to Be Known as Common Knowledge: What They Thought and What They Have Left] 常識として知っておきたい世界の哲学者50人：彼らは何を考え、私たちに何を残したのか？. Tokyo: Kawade Shobo Shinsha 河出書房新社, 2006.

The List of the First Appearance

* To Live in Belief   —*The Silver Coach*—
First Appearance: *Maho no Empitsu* 16 (1997)
* Seeking for an Eternal Companion   —from *Emily, the Liar*—
First Appearance: *Maho no Empitsu* 17 (1998)
* What Mice Suggest to Us   —The Creatures That Dwell in Another World—
First Appearance: *Maho no Empitsu* 18 (1999)
* Imagination and Freedom   —Ability the Mousewife Acquired—
First Appearance: *Maho no Empitsu* 19 (2000)
* From Being a Benefactor to Being a Friend   —*The Cat Visitor*—
First Appearance: *Maho no Empitsu* 20 (2001)
* Longing for Eternity   I   —What Has Arisen from the World of Lindgren's Works—
First Appearance: *Maho no Empitsu* 21 (2002)
* Longing for Eternity   II   —"The Eternal Child" in Lindgren—
First Appearance: *Maho no Empitsu* 22 (2003)
* Building Up an Image of an Independent Woman   —What Does *The Yearling* Mean to Rawlings?—
First Appearance: *Maho no Empitsu* 23 (2004)
* The Ability of Severance and the Future   —*Ai's Left Side*—
First Appearance: *Maho no Empitsu* 24 (2005)
* In the Garden of Integration and Restoration   —What Is the Significance of *The Secret Garden* to Burnett?—
First Appearance: *Maho no Empitsu* 25 (2006)
* The Two in the Haze   —Why was *Peter Pan* Born?—
First Appearance: *Maho no Empitsu* 26 (2007)
* From an Incomprehensible Story to a Comprehensible Story   —*Tom's Midnight Garden* by Philippa Pearce—
First Appearance: *Maho no Empitsu* 27 (2008)
* The Negative Aspects in Human Nature   —Comparing the Two Editions of Japanese Translation of *The Hundred Dresses* by Eleanor Estes—
First Appearance: *Criticism on Children's Literature* published by Tobirano-kai (2009)
* The Man Who Wanted to Become a King   —*The Little Prince* and *The Wisdom of the Sands* as Its Parent Body—
First Appearance: *Maho no Empitsu* 30 (2011)

Afterword

Children's Literature for Adults

I once read a foreign novel which featured a middle-aged prostitute, who led an untidy and harsh life. It is a romance, in which a young man loves her irresistibly. What is impressing is that she cleans up only her bathroom. The bathroom might be what is called "the last bastion," which she wants to keep clean, or which she doesn't want anyone to spoil. That is, the bathroom seems to embody her soul. After making a great fuss, she, to my surprise, enters college and majors in children's literature. The reason is not explained in the novel. I recall the adult novel at times, maybe because its development was incomprehensible.

I assume that she wanted to live her life again from the start. Before she meets the young man, she often closeted herself in the bathroom and washed it crystal clean, and then bathed, after having had an unpleasant experience. This behavior might indicate her wish to keep her true self clean, whatever might be true of her appearance.

This year, I had a maintenance worker glass-coat the walls, the ceiling and the floor of our bathroom stained with mold, spending a considerable amount of money. Thanks to this maintenance, a cloud which had stayed in my head for a long time disappeared. They guaranteed that the bathroom would be free of mold for ten years. A young worker did that job. It took him a long time, from nine am. till ten pm., to bleach, sterilize, wash and glass-coat the bathroom larger than ordinary ones. Although it might have been a lot of hard work for him, it ended in creating good relationships between my son and me and the man, who joined our dinner, eating food for my husband, who had warned that he would be home late. We enjoyed a pleasant talk.

Every time I wipe off the water over the walls and the floor of the bathroom with the towel as it needs cleaning, I recollect the day. It might be because it was an experience which reminded me of the scene in the novel.

Shiori Sato
Dec. 28, 2015
Sapporo

To the English Edition

Thirty-five years has passed since I became fascinated by overseas children's literature. In these stories adults stand next to and behind the boy or girl protagonist, and the adults are deeply related to the protagonists. I have been particularly concerned about the women. As they are often closely connected to the protagonists as their wives or mothers, their struggles to be true to themselves in their lives appealed to me from the space between the lines. I wanted to make their voices clearer.

I, as a Japanese woman, have observed the stifling life of women through the lives of my grandmother and my mother. In reading the novels dealt with in this book, I found this was also common to the lives of women in other countries. I focused on them in writing my essays on criticism on children's books. When they accumulated I decided to publish a book. I realized that this was what I have wanted. Soon, a wish emerged in me like a flame that my essays may be read by the women overseas and they may share my thoughts. I wanted to make the most of the fact that it is a book about overseas literary works. Fortunately, I could find a translator who would help my dream come true.

For a long time I have looked up to Hayao Kawai, a Jungian psychologist, as my preceptor. He is thought to have contributed to letting the rivers from the West and the East meet. I wish to follow in his footsteps, even if my progress might be so small.

This English edition would not have been born without the dedication by Ms. Misae Saso, the chief editor of Terrainc, who has realized my dream of publishing an English version of my book, which might have been impossible without her help, and Ms. Ritsuko Hirose, who has translated my Japanese into beautiful English, looking for perfectly fitting words, one by one. I am deeply grateful to them. And, at the same time, I am sure that this publication will lead us three to the acquisition of new freedom.

Shiori Sato
Dec. 1, 2015
Sapporo

Afterword by the Translator

When Ms. Sato asked me at a children's literature study meeting to translate into English her newly published essays on criticism on children's literature, I hesitated to accept her offer, considering the situation of my family and wondering whether I was competent enough. However, I accepted it, being moved by her earnest wish to know how non-Japanese would evaluate her works. Adding to that, I thought this would be a good opportunity for me, as a student of English and British children's literature, to apply what I have learnt and help connect people who are interested in children's literature both from Japan and other countries. I am thankful for the encounter with Ms. Sato.

    The process of translation, reading the words, one by one, or interpreting what the writer meant to write, and putting them into appropriate expressions in English was interesting and exciting, but sometimes a hard work. In that process, I was captured by her enthusiastic approach toward the subjects of her research, in which she revealed her innate personal motives to write, or confronted the works and the authors as issues of her own. She says that many of the essays took her one year to finish. In the English edition, only the books referred to in the text are listed at the end of each chapter, but the lists in the original book show her vast reading.

The title of this book, "becoming free" expresses Ms. Sato's mind. She says that Rumer Godden's *The Mousewife* is the book she loves most. Just as the mousewife gradually becomes free by gaining the ability to imagine, to Ms. Sato, the process of writing the essays on criticism on children's literature might be part of the process of becoming free.

I hope her thoughts reach readers around the world.

Ritsuko Hirose
Dec. 20, 2015
Sapporo

Profiles

AUTHOR
Shiori Sato

was born in 1952 in Setana-cho, Kudo-gun, Hokkaido. She graduated from The Center for Research in Picture Books and Children's Literature in the 6th graduating year. She became a member of Maho-no-Empitsu [Magic Pencil], a society for research in children's literature, in 1997 and Tobira no Kai [The Door], a society for criticism on children's literature, in 2002. She published *Jiyu ni Natteiku* [Becoming Free] as a private edition in 2010, and it was published by Terrainc, in 2013. This book was registered as a set book by Japan Library Association. She lives in Sapporo.

TRANSLATOR
Ritsuko Hirose

earned a bachelor's degree in English Literature from Japan Women's University in 1966 and a master's degree in Children's Literature from Roehampton University (UK) in 2011. She became a member of Mayu [Cocoon], a society for research in children's culture and literature, in 1980 and The Japan Society for Children's Literature in English in 2004. She translated picture books drawn by Yuriko Oido, *The Island Where Ororon, Common Murres, Fly* (2009), written by Michiko Ochi, *A Brook in Winter* (2010) with a poem written by Shigeru Seki, and *Oido-zakura, Cherry Trees* (2013) written by Yuriko Oido, which were published by Smoke House (Sapporo). She lives in Sapporo.

ILLUSTRATOR
Sayuri Yamada

published *Bea Ojisan no Kantan Oyatsu* [Uncle Bear's Sweet Cooking] (Sapporo: Johokikaku, 2003) and *Torikaekko Shiyo* [Let's Exchange] (picture book, Tokyo: Suzuki Shuppan, 2010). She lives in Sapporo.

■作:佐藤　栞（さとう・しおり）

札幌在住。

1952年　北海道久遠郡せたな町生まれ。

1996年　特定非営利活動法人　絵本、児童文学研究センター　第六期卒業。

1997年〜　児童文学研究会「まほうのえんぴつ」同人。

2002年〜　「児童文学批評．扉の会」同人。

（著書）

『自由になっていく』（2010年）

『自由になっていく』（てらいんく、2013年）　※日本図書館協会選定図書

■訳:廣瀬律子（ひろせ・りつこ）

札幌在住。

「まゆ児童文学会」（室蘭）同人。

「日本イギリス児童文学会」会員。

1966年　日本女子大学英文学科卒業

2011年　ローハンプトン大学（イギリス）児童文学修士号取得

（翻訳）

絵本『オロロンとぶ鳥』（文・越智道子、絵・大井戸百合子、スモークハウス、2009年）

絵本『ふゆのおがわ』（詩・関しげる、絵・大井戸百合子、曲・越智道子、スモークハウス、2010年）

絵本『大井戸ざくら』（文・絵・大井戸百合子、スモークハウス、2013年）

■表紙・イラスト:山田白百合（やまだ・さゆり）

イラストレーター。札幌在住。

（著書）

『ベアおじさんのかんたんおやつ』（情報企画、2003年）

絵本『とりかえっこしよう！』（鈴木出版、2010年）

◆てらいんくの評論

英文版　児童文学評論集　自由になっていく
BECOMING FREE

発行日	2016 年 9 月 28 日　初版第一刷発行
著　者	佐藤　栞
訳　者	廣瀬　律子
装挿画	山田白百合
発行者	佐相美佐枝
発行所	株式会社てらいんく
	〒 215-0007　神奈川県川崎市麻生区向原 3-14-7
	TEL　044-953-1828　　FAX　044-959-1803
	振替　00250-0-85472
印刷所	株式会社厚徳社

ⓒ Shiori Sato 2013
English translation ⓒ Ritsuko Hirose 2016
Printed in Japan
ISBN978-4-86261-123-9　C0095

定価はカバーに表示してあります。
落丁・乱丁のお取り替えは送料小社負担でいたします。
購入書店名を明記のうえ、直接小社制作部までお送りください。
本書の一部または全部を無断で複写・複製・転載することを禁じます。